Hermeneutics, Metacognition, and Writing

Edited by
Dr. Maryann P. DiEdwardo
Lehigh University;
University of Maryland Global Campus

Series in Literary Studies

VERNON PRESS

www.vernonpress.com

In the Americas:
Vernon Press
1000 N West Street,
Suite 1200, Wilmington,
Delaware 19801
United States

In the rest of the world:
Vernon Press
C/Sancti Espiritu 17,
Malaga, 29006
Spain

Series in Literary Studies

Library of Congress Control Number: 2019950400

ISBN: 978-1-64889-027-7

Also available: 978-1-62273-822-9 [Hardback]; 978-1-62273-909-7 [PDF, E-Book]

What Others Have Said about
Hermeneutics, Metacognition, and Writing

"In her collection of essays featuring the work of literary giants like Toni Morrison and Emily Dickinson, editor Maryann DiEdwardo and her contributors map out the terrain of grief and injustice, and make convincing arguments about the efficacy of literature to heal wounds. These ambitious essays are at once erudite, engaging, and remarkably hopeful."

—Stephanie Powell Watts

(Stephanie Powell Watts won the Ernest J. Gaines Award for Literary Excellence for her debut story collection, *We Are Taking Only What We Need* (2012), also named one of 2013's Best Summer Reads by *O, The Oprah Magazine*.)

"Patti Pasda, as artist, is a painter of animals, especially horses, and it is obvious that she is attuned to their free spirits. As a person in the community, she is equally engaged and understanding, whether she is interacting with an individual or supporting action for global betterment. Patti Pasda—courageous, loyal, loving."

—Professor Emeritus John F. Vickrey
Lehigh University

Reviews about Dr. Maryann Pasda DiEdwardo's Books

The Fourth "R": A Book to Promote the Journey Through Hispanic American Literary History to Develop Language Skills, and *Music Transforms the College English Classroom*

"Dr. DiEdwardo's books are must-haves for all educators, especially for those who teach students of other languages. The book is simple and its components are easy to follow. What I find particularly compelling about this book is the idea to use authors from the students' home country to enhance self-esteem and pride, in addition to creating individual voices."

—Toni Velleca, ESOL teacher

To

Friederike Victoria "Joy" Adamson
January 20, 1910–January 3, 1980

and

Chloe Ardelia Wofford "Toni" Morrison
February 18, 1931–August 5, 2019

and

Virginia McKenna

Table of Contents

Preface

Our book presents a theme and a focus on interpretation through writing, film, poetry, and action. On September 26, 2019, I attended a lecture by Virginia McKenna in New York City, where she stated that "animals should live in the wild" (McKenna).

In a gentle rain, I walked toward the White Space in Chelsea. I approached the venue. But when I noticed Virginia standing with a group of people, I approached her to share my story.

In the Chelsea section of Manhattan, I meet Virginia Anne McKenna, OBE, born June 7, 1931, a British stage and screen actress, author, and wildlife campaigner. She is best known for her films and books. She co-founded *Born Free* in 1984. The Born Free Foundation is an international charity organization.

My first meeting with the British actress, author, and conservationist captivates. With her son, she speaks about the reason for animals to be free to live in the wild. They discuss the importance of a short film campaign to raise awareness of the exploitation of South Africa's lions. The film is titled *The Bitter Bond*.

She inspires and supports compassionate conservation which puts the welfare of individual animals at the heart of effective conservation actions. The Virginia McKenna Award for Compassionate Conservation is named in honor of Virginia McKenna.

Dr. Maryann P. DiEdwardo

Works Cited

McKenna, Virginia. "A Night for Wildlife." White Space, Chelsea, New York City, New York, 26 Sept. 2019.

Figure 1. Maryann P. DiEdwardo, Virginia McKenna, and Patricia Pasda at an event in New York, NY, by the Born Free Foundation, on Thursday, September 26, 2019. Photo used with permission of Patricia Gould.

Editor's Acknowledgments

This book owes much to our friends, colleagues, and discourse communities. Our project grew from conversations with the contributors over the years in addition to academic participation at conferences. Many thanks to the Northeast Modern Language Association for selecting me to chair a panel at the 2019 NeMLA annual conference in Washington, DC. I am grateful to Vernon Press for their interest in a new book based on conference panel themes, and to the Vernon production staff for their continuing support of this project.

Our conference presenters' and invited scholars' generous contributions to this project are invaluable: Dr. Juliet Emanuel, Jill Kroeger Kinkade, Dr. T. Madison Peschock, Susan Stangeland, and of course, my sister Patricia J. Pasda.

Thanks to Vivien L. Steele and Nancy Seidenberger for their pre-publication reading, to Shirley A. Emanuel for her participation as a reviewer, to Professor Emeritus John F. Vickrey for his compassion and lifelong commitment to scholarship, to Professor Stephanie Powell Watts for her friendship and support, and to Joseph A. DiEdwardo for sharing his diverse talents and encouraging me throughout this process.

I thank my husband Amedeo for his patience and understanding forever.

List of Illustrations

Editor's Introduction

The story of the formation of *Hermeneutics, Metacognition, and Writing* begins with the study of English. In 1975, Dr. Maryann P. DiEdwardo graduated, summa cum laude, from the Department of Arts and Architecture at The Pennsylvania State University, as the recipient of the Carnegie Scholarship for academic excellence. She received a Fellowship in 1976 to study writing at Lehigh University, where she still teaches as an adjunct professor for the Graduate School of Computer Science and Engineering. The Center for Teaching and Learning at Lehigh University invited her to lecture on "Hermeneutics, Metacognition, and Writing" at the 2019 Symposium held at Lehigh University. The lecture was titled "Hermeneutics, Metacognition, and Writing." A critique is hermeneutic. Writing combines hermeneutics in action and metacognitive ideology. *Hermeneutics, Metacognition, and Writing* investigates the useful social functionality of actions of essential criteria of study. Text, respect for history by the author of the text, and consideration of the significance of the text move toward the goal of praxis. Hermeneutic arcs are useful to organize and interpret information in order to prepare critiques. The intersectionality of hermeneutics, metacognition, and semiotics, as well as cultural poetics, uses cultural heritage. The takeaway initiates self-monitoring as metacognition, or meta-reflection.

My sister and co-author (refer to "Bibliography of Works and List of Presentations") Patricia Pasda contacted the Born Free Foundation, an international charity organization, and Born Free U.S.A., to gather knowledge about the quest for a global literacy program based on the goals presented in her paper connected to the newest research studies on conservation and the work of Joy Adamson. This book will support conservation through the devotion of Patricia Pasda to seek international networks where we can, as sisters, to work on continuing the work of Joy Adamson to promote compassionate conservation. We intend to reach a global audience and to extend our book as a way to speak for all humans and those creatures that have no voice.

Your gift of buying our book supports our global literacy project. We visit schools, community centers, and hospitals, as well as spaces where we will gather hope for peacefulness and generosity. Our project goals include global literacy and compassionate conservation as a world community. This book supports Born Free U.S.A. and the Born Free Foundation, an international charity organization.

Patricia presented her paper, "The Development and Impact of Joy Adamson's Work with Lions in Africa," for our panel in Washington, DC, in 2019 (chapter 4). She writes the following: "Therefore, in the hermeneutics approach, the cause of Joy's success with Elsa's freedom was Joy's firm belief in Elsa's right to live free, and this snowballed through each person exposed to Joy's work, into the great conservation effort we have and desperately need to keep vibrant today. Nearly five hundred of Joy Adamson's paintings are preserved and on display in the Joy Adamson museum in Nairobi, Kenya, for she is the recognized mother of African conservation" (Patricia Pasda, chapter 4). In chapter 4, Patricia draws from the right strands of literature. She uses primary and secondary sources for a qualitative essay and appropriately acknowledges prior academic literature. Patricia's illustrations, figures 2 and 3, are copies of a letter from Joy Adamson to Patricia, printed with permission. The letter and envelope are in her private collection. Patricia points out that it is vital for the reader to understand that Kenya is the place where (Nairobi, Kenya, Adamson museum) Joy Adamson is recognized as the mother of African conservation (Nairobi, Kenya, Adamson museum). The author also points out the importance of the study of hermeneutic philosophy in the field of conservation, which can apply to human emotion such as kindness to animals. Patricia tells us that the approach was why Joy Adamson was so successful. The project goals include global literacy and compassionate conservation as a world community. Hermeneutics is practice and theory of interpretation, understanding, and respect for history by the author. The result of this extension, or interpolation, is to deepen and clarify a thought path begun by Ricoeur. His model of interpretation and critique integrates discourse within a respect for human experience and action that emphasizes the creative and imaginative uses of language.

Hermeneutics specifically applies to interpretation, usually of Scripture. Exegesis, often used with textual analysis of Scripture, refers to the analysis of any text. Practical applications of this science and art of interpretation has been DiEdwardo's research methodology for conducting case studies and writing research papers for the Lilly Conference on Evidence Based Pedagogy, College English Association (CEA), Northeast Modern Language Association International Conferences (NeMLA), Southern Atlantic Modern Language Association (SaMLA), Lehigh University, and the University of Maryland Global Campus lectures (UMGC), as well as Multi-Ethnic Literature of the United States (MELUS), articles, and published books. In 2018, Dr. Maryann P. DiEdwardo was selected as chair for a panel for the Northeast Modern Language Association Convention to be held in 2019. The theme was "Transnational Spaces: Intersections of Cultures, Languages, and Peoples." Upon publishing the "Call for Papers" to present the papers in 2019 in

Washington, DC, she was contacted about a new book based on the panel themes. Subsequently, Maryann contracted with Vernon Press to craft a book.

Dr. Maryann P. DiEdwardo, Patricia Pasda, and Dr. T. Madison Peschock presented papers at the NeMLA in Washington, DC. DiEdwardo's presentation was "Social Justice and Cultural Landscape: Toni Morrison's *Beloved*" (chapter 6). Dr. T. Madison Peschock presented chapter 5, "Mrs. Hitchcock's Coming Out Party – The Injustice to Women in Hitchcock's Life Revealed in Films." Peschock reevaluates the director Alfred Hitchcock and reflects on his injustice to women.

DiEdwardo also writes chapter 1, "The Intersectionality of Hermeneutics, Metacognition, and Semiotics"; in chapter 3, "Social Movements: Frank Bidart, Zora Neale Hurston, and Jack Kerouac," she investigates social movements; she also contributes chapter 7, "Metacognitive Pedagogy Breaks Down Interpersonal Borders"; and chapter 11, "Narrative Hermeneutics." In chapter 13, "New Utterances, the Overmind, and Moments of Being: Three Modernists Reach Beyond Ordinary Consciousness," Jill Kroeger Kinkade presents her research investigating three writers who explore consciousness in their fiction and nonfiction works: D. H. Lawrence, Hilda Doolittle (hereafter H.D.), and Virginia Woolf.

Biblical hermeneutics: DiEdwardo contributes chapter 2, "Exegesis of St. Maximilian Maria Kolbe and Thomas Merton."

Chapter 8, **"Biblical Hermeneutics and the Book of Job"** was written by Susan Stangeland, an interfaith minister who offers her expertise and scholarship in the area of Biblical hermeneutics. The author has taken great care to clearly define the time frame in which the Book of Job takes place. The strands of literature the author uses are appropriate, having to do with biblical hermeneutics and they define and prove the author's thesis and research. This research is drawn from academic sources and organized in a logical fashion, with conclusions from scholarly study. The writer's ability to guide the reader through the Book of Job explains both the antagonist and the protagonist points of view. Clearly presented, this writing will be understood by theologians, academics, and readers of many ages. The writing piece is consistent and clear, requiring no use of tables or illustrated timelines. The reader will emerge with a better understanding of Job and his world.

Chapter 10, "Francis of Assisi, A Tale of a Dog, and Hermeneutics" is by Patricia Pasda.

Case study research

Contributions of two case study researchers include Dr. Maryann P. DiEdwardo's "The Poetic Vision of Emily Dickinson: A Case Study" in chapter

12, and Dr. Juliet Emanuel's four case studies which answer significant questions linking hermeneutics, metacognition, and writing in chapter 9, "Reflections from a Reading Classroom."

Chapter 14 is the "conclusion," a memorial to Toni Morrison, to inspire radical compassion. This researcher advocates evidence-based change through service writing, volunteering at local and regional as well as national community engagement events, for promoting human rights.

This book focuses on hermeneutics, interpretation, and the philosophy of metacognition. Writing fuses into a learning community for reflection. DiEdwardo embraces research in action in applications of a case study for chapter 12 of this book. She focuses on three attributes of hermeneutical arc including text, explanation of the text, and understanding in reflections. For example, imagine new insights into the meaning of the poetry of Emily Dickinson for applications of reading poetry for healing from grief. In anticipation of exploring reading the poetry of Emily Dickinson as a therapy, one may read poems by Dickinson, reflecting upon the poems, and writing poetry. The most important outcome of hermeneutics and metacognition in writing is cultural poetics, which seeks to identify literary works as social discourses. Crafting original poetry and reflections in a journal prepare this researcher to write. The poetry uses metaphors and imagery from the single subject's experiences as she relates to her sadness over the deaths of her parents. Exposure to poetry for the single subject, in a concentrated set of activities (actions) and scheduled study times (spaces), was helpful. She recognized her grief. Reading, reflecting, and writing poetry was an approach to engage in interpreting the self to create poetic and aesthetic praxis. The limitations are the shortness of reflections and poems by the single subject. The case study may only observe the single subject. The results of the case study reveal that the researcher reinvents her devotion to the study of poetry.

Further, metacognition supports the paradigm of active learning. Writers possess qualities of memory based on human everyday experiences, similar to those experiences within literary works they read. Use life story writing next to recount experiences that may help them find a thesis. Write for a global multiethnic and ageless audience. Stories can indeed reach all readers. Play podcasts of sample student essays that show how students recall events. Metacognition, student-directed pedagogical models, and 21st-century pop culture themes fuse to ignite a learning community for reflection, discovery, and social networking to motivate the 21st-century student. The class is themed on ideas about the human condition. Students create journals as primary sources for essays. Writing based on keen observation and self-discovery is a part of learning to write. Students will need to find ways to enjoy the pace by excelling in their writing from the first week. Paradigms of research-based internet resources like Diigo are useful to create annotated bibliographies to collect data.

Shirley A. Emanuel explains a case study titled "Reflections from a Reading Classroom" by an invited scholar:

> This essay begins with a question. The answer invites the reader into the classroom to experience a journey. A journey which includes the impact of past trauma on learning. It exemplifies the development and evolution of trusting relationships, between students and writer, which were necessary to the provision and acceptance of the learning and teaching tools used by the writer. The tools motivated and enabled the students to utilize self-exploration, build self-confidence and self-trust resulting in the mastery and proficiency of language.
>
> Shirley A. Emanuel

In creating social justice praxis, we connect key themes of social justice literacy with writers and writing. Social justice as a paradigm for the English classroom resounds with tension and resolution. Gandhi protested against racism in South Africa and colonial rule in India by using nonviolent resistance. A testament to the revolutionary power of nonviolence, Gandhi's approach directly influenced Martin Luther King Jr. Kingian Principles establish further study of social justice literacy.

Global Literacy, a multicultural study, is practical and timely. We develop information literacy skills. We use research and composing for inquiry, learning, critical thinking, and communicating in various rhetorical contexts, and develop the habit of locating, evaluating, and ethically and persuasively using primary and secondary research materials. We engage in facility with argument. Through the study of rhetoric, we anticipate the needs of various audiences, understand the basic conventions of chosen genres, and analyze and adapt to varying rhetorical situations. Weeks 1 and 2 include writing argument summary exploratory essays. Weeks 3 and 4 emphasize the research question. Weeks 5, 6, 7, 8, 9, and 10 involve writing a research paper. Weeks 11, 12, 13, 14, and 15: Choice 1. Menu, poster, WordPress to present with a team of one or more, to share research in the area of themes we address in class; or, Choice 2. Short documentary film. YouTube. Create your own.

Purpose

Conclusively, this book seeks to develop empathy. The researcher juxtaposes post-structuralism and postmodern philosophical paradigms. She intertwines critical hermeneutics. The evidence of the text itself, as a creative space, constructs an imagined cultural landscape where we find radical compassion, hope, and human rights.

Dr. Maryann P. DiEdwardo

Works Cited

Emanuel, Shirley A. "Thanks to Shirley A. Emanuel for her participation." Message to Maryann DiEdwardo. September 8, 2019. Email.

Chapter 1

The Intersectionality of Hermeneutics, Metacognition, and Semiotics

Dr. Maryann P. DiEdwardo

Lehigh University;
University of Maryland Global Campus

Hermeneutics, Metacognition, and Writing investigates the useful social functionality of actions of essential criterion of hermeneutic study. Text, respect for history by the author of the text, and consideration of the significance of the text move toward the goal of praxis. Hermeneutic arcs are useful to organize and interpret information to prepare critiques. The intersectionality of hermeneutics, metacognition, and semiotics, as well as cultural poetics, uses cultural heritage. The takeaway initiates self-monitoring as metacognition, or meta-reflection. One interprets literature to signify social change: therefore, one can consider literature as a social discourse. The meaning of social discourse is a conversation about freedoms such as the abilities to speak and to voice opinions for the purpose of human rights. To prepare for this book and to engage in primary source research for a qualitative research study, this researcher performed a case study research project. The importance, therefore, in experiencing the aesthetic of the writing of poetry is one of literary hermeneutics. Unlike classical philology, literary hermeneutics will not only consider the aesthetic character of the text to be interpreted in an evaluation which follows from interpretation, but it will make the aesthetic character a premise of the interpretation itself.

Intersectionality of history as well as poetics and aesthetics frame this researcher's case study. Therefore, we accept that there is a consciousness of historicity which is suggested by Peter Szondi and Timothy Bahti, as in "Introduction to Literary Hermeneutics" (Szondi and Bahti 20). Additionally, let us ask the following question that will be the theme of a case study by this researcher. Can one heal from grief by reading the poetry of Emily Dickinson? Criterion for interpretation through the study and philosophy of Aristotle reflects and questions fundamental assumptions (Malpas et al.). The future of hermeneutics may be modeled with an understanding of poetic and aesthetic praxis. The results of Maryann DiEdwardo's case study reveal that respect for the history of the poetic vision of Dickinson, reflection upon her works, and creative original poetry combine inquiry and systematic methods of interpretation. DiEdwardo's case study embraces hermeneutics in action. From the perspective of hermeneutic interpretation, consider the impact of writing journal entries of short reflections and poetry as a methodology to create personal and poetic embodied space, the location where human experience and consciousness take on material and spatial form. Apply a hermeneutic approach to interpret poetry by writing original poetry. The actions of the essential criterion of hermeneutic study use text, respect for history by the author of the text, and consideration of the significance of the text.

Perhaps, according to editor Lorraine Code, in *Feminist Interpretations of Hans-Georg Gadamer*, published by Pennsylvania University Press, 2003, a feminist inquiry offers wider horizons for philosophers … (337). Methodology in the case study uses the poetry of Dickinson for inquiry and interpretation of the events and conditions of daily life. By doing so, Dr. M. DiEdwardo relies on Plato, who uses knowledge as a spiritual endeavor, revealed and intuitive. Support of previous research includes "A Hermeneutics of Contemplative Silence: Paul Ricoeur and the Heart of Meaning" by Michelle Therese Kueter Petersen. She joins the process of description, explanation, and interpretation with the traditional religious journey (Peterson 1).

The most important outcome of hermeneutics and metacognition in writing is cultural poetics which seeks to identify literary works as social discourses. Crafting original poetry and reflections in a journal prepared this researcher to write. The poetry uses metaphors and imagery from the single subject's experiences as she relates to her sadness over the deaths of her parents. She recognized her grief. Reading, reflecting, and writing poetry was an approach to engage in interpreting the self to create poetic and aesthetic praxis. The limitations are the shortness of reflections and poems by the single subject. The case study may only observe the single subject. The results of the case study reveal that the researcher reinvents her devotion to the study of poetry.

Further, researchers write critiques to practice hermeneutic planning. The framework as a prewriting exercise allows us to use critical reading skills to enhance writing activity. Reading to doubt, or exploratory writing, offers reflective writing practices to discover style and personal voice or alternative topics. Thinking about literature through the lens of the hermeneutic arc with metacognitive activities may enlighten us to better writing. In fact, this researcher promotes the use of metacognition to begin the outlines for the research, and finally, cultural poetics to see the literary work as a social discourse. Investigating the useful social functionality of literature, as well as the theoretical processes of the literary scholar, regards the power of writing for cultural change. "Hermeneutic Approach for Conducting Literature Reviews and Literature Searches" by Sebastian K. Boeil and Dubravka Cecez-Kecmnanoc inspires us. The authors propose a hermeneutic framework that integrates analysis and interpretation of literature and the search for literature. Furthermore, the authors explain two circles: the search and acquisition circle and analysis and interpretation circle (Boeil et al.). Studying previously researched knowledge, whether within Scripture or secular contexts, constitutes a text, a respect for history by the author of the text, and the significance of the text, and participate in a study that will lead to understanding appropriate approaches to writing about the text. The hermeneutic arc offers us a methodology for interpretation. "Hermeneutics, in France as elsewhere abroad, is frequently associated with the work of Paul Ricoeur" (Frey viii). Researchers accomplish understanding by explanation, understanding, and appropriation, which Ricoeur called the hermeneutic arc. Explanation explores the nature of the text; understanding explores the question, which the text presents; and appropriation, interpreting the text for oneself, expands knowledge and perception. Jeff Malpas and Hans-Helmuth Gander, editors of *The Routledge Companion to Hermeneutics*, establish hermeneutic origins; explain thinkers; ask questions; describe engagements, challenges, and dialogues; and conclude with the future of hermeneutics.

Strategies based on metacognition engage memories of readings, life experiences, and imagination. Accordingly, these three patterns compose voice.

Modern hermeneutics includes both verbal and nonverbal communications as well as semiotics, presuppositions, and pre-understandings. Metacognitive processes focus on learning with self-discovery in hard-copy journals. Writing assignments ask us to take positions on cultural issues or questions of interpretation. Combine metacognition and hermeneutic models to ask how a particular effect is achieved or why an ending seems right, but also what a particular line means and what a literary work tells us about the human condition. Critical hermeneutics is an approach to transform readers. Considering the impact that researchers make on their readers, we can change the researcher with hermeneutics, metacognition, and cultural poetics to illuminate the necessity for textual interpretation beyond texts, through exploration, understanding, and appropriation. Objectives are to achieve a cultural interest in the methods we use to reflect, construct, and mediate experiences in the world. Social justice as a paradigm resounds with tension and resolution dependent on the silent resilience of the individual. The framework short story fuses our concentration on signs and interpretation as a focus to envision the writers in a creative process to offer transformation. Globalization of the literary canon requires applications of the aspects of oral history traditions. To write, this researcher engages memories of readings, life experiences, and imagination. Accordingly, these three patterns compose voice on the written page. As cultures converge in the global 21st century, writers of multiethnic backgrounds require varied models to succeed. Reading, writing, and arithmetic, which served our industrial society, may be enhanced by a new fourth "R," or remembrance, as the educational focus for the age of technology and multiculturalism. Language is the basis of classrooms, whether traditional, enhanced, or distance. Students read the works of multicultural authors and create audio presentations on YouTube. Music, photography, art, and Netflix become the new literature that enhances learning. Stories that students create in the new literature of the social network become the new voices for a global cultural literature revolution.

Through the lens of hermeneutics and semiotics, consider the cultural poetics in the film *Roma*. Director Alfonso Cuaron portrays the injustice and suffering of the main character, Cleo. He engages viewers to explore archetypical cultural milieu Mexico in 1970. Interpretation of texts is the main purpose of hermeneutics. However, through semiotics as an additional theoretical model, we can study film as well. Semiotics is the study of signs. Moreover, as a reflective inquiry, hermeneutics or the study of aletheia, the Greek word for "unhiddenness," reveals truth (Moules). Through the use of the hermeneutic arc, this researcher interprets literary works and film as visual literature. Interpretation of current films such as *Roma*, directed by Alfonso Cuaron, tells the story of Cleo, a domestic worker who experiences the death of her child. Cleo helps take care of the children of Antonio and Sofia. The story is complex since Antonia suddenly runs away with his mistress. The story unfolds as Cleo becomes pregnant with the child of a cousin of a friend. When she tells him of her upcoming pregnancy, he threatens to kill her and the baby. Yet, the baby is stillborn. Cleo goes on a vacation to the beach and experiences healing when she saves two children from drowning in the ocean. Cleo is a character that embodies the life of a servant who does not have rights in the society, but who has found a caring employer during the 1970s in Mexico. The audience feels empathy for Cleo, who is mute after the loss of her child. Cuaron directs a passionate cast in a heart-wrenching film which we interpret as a social discourse. Cultural landscape, which portrays the places in the film, is also significant. Cleo uses water to clean as a metaphor for the place and space that she portrays in the film. She has not experienced human rights in her relationship with her child's father.

What is metacognition? Metacognition is thinking about thinking. John H. Flavell coined the term "metacognition" in the seventies of the last century (Flavell). In the book published in 2013, called *Reflection and Using Metacognition to Improve Student Writing*, editors Matthew Kaplan, Naomi Silver, Danielle Lavaque-Mantz, and Deborah Meizlish provide a template for a new writing environment. Blended-learning approaches use the three attributes of this hermeneutical including text, explanation of the text, and understanding in reflections. As an example, we select the text *Using Reflection and Metacognition to Improve Student Learning*, specifically chapter 8, "Reflection, e-portfolios, and WEPO." The authors suggest that social pedagogy based on writing and editing, in print and online, adds valuable experiences for writers. The text is carefully written. This researcher interprets the evidence that the authors present as valid. Readers also experienced the use of the social pedagogy. A text and a clear explanation in both a word processing program and a website or digital humanities for the 21st-century writing student. This researcher uses a storyboard to aid the writer in understanding writing and editing in print and online. Film aesthetic provides a backdrop to us as writers. Ethos, logos, and pathos exist within the characters and are also present in the setting; use interpretation to evolve as writers.

In 2017, this researcher published an article titled "Implementing Learning Strategies Based on Metacognition" in the *Journal of Modern Education Review*. She presents learning strategies based on metacognition, or thinking about thinking. The planning of a writing project "centers upon activities that support preparation to act as cognitive mappers to create new literature of the social network as new voices for a global cultural revolution" (DiEdwardo 380). Stories that writers create in the new literature of the social network become the new voices for a global cultural literature revolution. By telescoping into a shorter version of oral history, writers succeed in the learning community.

At the 2019 Symposium at Lehigh University, this researcher presented a lecture titled "Hermeneutics, Metacognition, and Writing." The intention of the event was to share a useful technological approach to writing. The purpose of the lecture identified the hermeneutic arc as a methodology to plan and implement research writing. The arc contains steps to interpret, understand, and appropriate the topic. Drafting begins with the critique. A critique is hermeneutic. Writing critiques combines hermeneutics in action and metacognitive ideology. The takeaway initiates self-monitoring as metacognition, or meta-reflection. Hermeneutics in action is practice and theory of interpretation, understanding, and respect for history by the author. The result of this extension, or interpolation, is to deepen understanding.

Further study in the area of critiques utilizes Diigo pages which contain links to books, articles, presentations, and published research. Coordinate Diigo resources with Google Scholar and library digital researches. Pursue broad questions that are fundamental to any efforts in research writing. Who is the author of the text? What period was the text about? How do we interpret the ideas? Hermenetutics has been useful as a way to interpret texts since antiquity and is called the hermeneutic circle. The critique is imperative. Hermeneutics discovers the impulse to critique, openness, and ... reasonableness in ethos (Weinsheimer, Preface). Critiques engage readers in analyzing key articles by scholars in the field, in blogs, wikis, websites, books, pamphlets, newsletters, journals, or other material demonstrating techniques of close reading in order to explicate a text with terms of the hermeneuticist, that apply to writing to converse, to analyze, and to use cultural heritage. Writers possess qualities of memory based on human everyday experiences similar to those experiences within literary works they read. Play podcasts of sample student essays that show how students recall events. Metacognition and 21st-century pop culture themes fuse to ignite us for reflection, discovery, and social networking. The critique is themed on ideas about the human condition. Create journals as primary sources for essays. Writing based on keen observation and self-discovery is a part of learning interpretation. Paradigms of research-based internet resources like Diigo are useful to create annotated bibliographies to collect data. Diigo as a resource is based on my own books, articles, presentations, and original published poetry. List other poets as well, especially 21st-century new poets.

Hermeneutics includes semiotics to signify transformation. Presuppositions, or previously successful or meditative reflective writing, with metacognition as a goal, refers to higher-order thinking which involves active control over the cognitive processes. Writers plan, evaluate, monitor, embed, inform, and train. In particular, the emphasis of writing online and in print formulates a writer's planning as a semiotic or significant stage of the writing process. Prewriting in an informal journal is metacognitive thinking in action. Metastudy means using previous skills in writing situations such as writing essays, outlines, online or hard copy journals. The e-portfolio suggests that we can collect ideas and reflect on the process of creation. The three attributes of this hermeneutical arc include text, explanation of the text, and understanding in reflections.

Charles Dickens teaches peace through his literature. He is an agent of change who adapts biblical allusions to teach morality. Hermeneutics of Dickens's works is a burgeoning field. His use of the Bible recaptures the essence of Christianity in his book *The Life of Our Lord* (Larson). This research seeks to apply critical hermeneutics, which takes nothing for granted. In fact, it is the taken-for-granted nature of understanding that is the object of study and, in particular, where that knowledge comes from. Hermeneutics stops at the point of saying that knowledge and understanding are historically and socially bound. Critical hermeneutics continues where traditional hermeneutics leaves off, by embarking on an examination of those social and historical conditions which make understanding possible.

This researcher refers to *The Life of Our Lord* by Charles Dickens as a way to investigate. The narrative gently tells the reader about the life of Christ and ends with the ultimate sadness of persecution of the Christians. Yet, the republished work is illustrated with Victorian-themed pictures to capture the cultural landscape of the Victorian Era. The book presents the life of Jesus Christ rewritten by Dickens for his children. The generous tone that Dickens applies in references to moral code shows radical compassion.

Why do writers write? "Social Justice, Thematic Tool and Paradigm in the Construction of the Novels of Dickens and DiEdwardo" was presented at the Hotel Bethlehem in April 2010 as part of the Pennsylvania College English Association Spring Conference called "English Studies and Social Justice." The answer is that characters, setting, mood, voice, and themes dynamically bring us to a state of relaxation and vision to understand truths. Literature is inspirational. My intention is to provide readers with tools to research the use of social justice as a reason to write and a methodology of applying the social justice paradigm for writing. Conclusively, this book seeks to develop empathy.

Works Cited

Boeil, Sebastian K., and Dubravka Cecez-Kecmanovic. "A Hermeneutic Approach for Conducting Literature Reviews and Literature Searches," *Communications of the Association for Information Systems*, vol. 34, article 12, pp. 57–286, Jan. 2014.

Code, Lorraine, editor. *Feminist Interpretations of Hans-Georg Gadamer*, University Park: Pennsylvania University Press, 2003.

DiEdwardo, Maryann P. *Diigo*. www.diigo.com/user/diedwardo7. Accessed 3 Oct. 2019.

---. "Implementing Learning Strategies Based on Metacognition." *Journal of Modern Education Review*, vol. 7, no. 6, June 2017, New York: Academic Start, 2017, pp. 380–388.

Flavell, J. H. "Metacognition and cognitive monitoring: A new area of cognitive-developmental inquiry. " *American Psychologist*, 34(10), 1987, pp. 906–911.

Frey, Daniel. Preface. Paul Ricoeur. *Hermeneutics, Writings and Lectures*, vol. 2. Trans. David Pellauer. Massachusetts: Malden, 2016.

Gadamer, Hans-Georg. Weinsheimer, Joel, trans. *Hermeneutics, Religion, and Ethics*. New Haven: Yale University Press, 1999.

Gander, Hans-Helmuth, Jeff Malpas, editors. *The Routledge Companion to Hermeneutics*. New York: Routledge, 2015.

Ghasemi, A., M. Taghinejad, A. Kabrini, and M. Imani. "Ricoeur's Theory of Interpretation: A Method for Understanding Text (Course Text)." *World Applied Science Journal 15* (11): pp. 1623–1629. IDOSI Publications, 2011.

Kaplan, Matthew, Naomi Silver, Danielle Lavaque-Mantz, and Deborah Meizlish, editors. *Reflection and Using Metacognition to Improve Student Learning*. Virginia: Stylus, 2013.

Larson, Janet L. "The Fractured Code in Dickens Fiction." *The Victorian Web*. www.victorianweb.org/authors/dickens/larson/1.html. 1 Aug. 2009.

Malpas, Jeff, and Hans-Gadamer, Hans-Georg. Weinsheimer, Joel. Trans. *Hermeneutics, Religion, and Ethics.* New Haven: Yale University Press, 1999.

Moules, Nancy J. "Hermeneutic Inquiry: Paying Heed to History and Hermes An Ancestral, Substantive, and Methodological Tale." *International Journal of Qualitative Methods,* Sept. 2002, pp. 1–21, doi:10.1177/160940690200100301. Accessed 3 Oct. 2019.

Petersen, Michele Therese Kueter. "A Hermeneutics of Contemplative Silence: Paul Ricoeur and the Heart of Meaning." *Iowa University Press Online.* Iowa City: University of Iowa Press, 2011.

Szondi, Peter, and Timothy Bahti. "Introduction to Literary Hermeneutics." *New Literary History,* vol. 10, no. 1, 1978, pp. 17–29. JSTOR, www.jstor.org/stable/468303. Accessed 3 Oct. 2019.

Chapter 2

Exegesis of St. Maximilian Maria Kolbe and Thomas Merton

Dr. Maryann P. DiEdwardo

Lehigh University;
University of Maryland Global Campus

Exegesis is a critical interpretation of a text. Apply lexical-syntactical analysis to look at words used and the way the words are used as well as literary analysis (Virkler and Ayayo 17). This researcher's study of the work of Maximilian Maria Kolbe began in 1993 after a period of serious illness. Healing from the illness may be due to a miracle which occurred after prayer and good works, which were the main activities, as well as devotions centered upon novenas to St. Kolbe. In 1982, Kolbe was declared a saint by Pope John Paul II. Upon entering married life in the same year, this researcher devoted her life to prayer. A set of devotional prayers by St. Kolbe were the early beginnings of my hermeneutic studies of Biblical readings from the liturgy of the hours, the prayers Christians perform daily. Let us look at Psalm 23 to find a methodology with a lens on the model of Augustine, who uses the fourfold sense of Scripture: the letter, the allegory, the moral, and the anagogy (Grant 119).

Exegesis of the writing of St. Maximilian Maria Kolbe and Thomas Merton is literary and reflective. Maximilian Maria Kolbe, a Franciscan friar, a martyr who was killed in a concentration camp to save another, provides a view of love that resembles the writing of Thomas Merton, a Trappist monk. A social critic and supporter of human rights, Thomas Merton, is an important writer in the American literary tradition. His explorations of religions of the East suggest interreligious dialogue. He was a writer and a Trappist monk. In the 1950s, Thomas published two books that dealt with the psalms: *Bread in the Wilderness* (1953) and a pamphlet titled *Praying the Psalms* (1956). Merton uses the psalms as allusions in his writing.

Franciscan friar Maximilian Kolbe and the Benedictine Trappist monk Thomas Merton serve as examples of seeking love through faith in God. *The Monastic Journey* by Thomas Merton, edited by Brother Patrick Hart, presents a background of research and hope for current 21st-century problems. Peace is still a concern worldwide. Merton suggests that there are three parts. The first section of the book recounts a definition of monastic vocation. Next, Merton considers monastic themes. Lastly, he explains the solitary life. We also apply literary analysis as a methodology (Virkler and Ayayo 2007). This researcher's study of the work of Thomas Merton, a Trappist monk, in international conferences about Merton's writing, also concentrates on the devotions of Merton to solitude and to prayer during times of despair. The writings of Merton are significant.

This essay acknowledges the study of Kolbe and Merton, in the 21st century, to further the joy of love as a goal to achieve peace. We begin with metacognitive preparation. Critical thinking results when we are prepared with cognitive strategies that give us empathy and self-reliance, so that we can seek pathos of inspiration and exegesis. In chapter 3, "Improving Critical-Thinking Skills in Introductory Biology Through Quality Practice and Metacognition," in *Using Reflection and Metacognition*, the authors argue that metacognition and critical thinking are separate constructs (Lipman 1988). The domains of text, action, and history are distinguished to represent the specific features of the research purpose (Ricoeur 9). The elements of writing research require preparation of the hermeneutic arc that we shall apply to the particular research question: How do hermeneutics of Scripture or of other texts about faith inspire us to love ourselves and others? The arc will consider love within the field of biblical hermeneutics. Love has origins in our own search for love. This chapter presupposes the nature of Revelation. Thanksgiving, supplication, and celebration are all engendered by what these movements of the heart allow to exist and to become manifest (Ricoeur). Love is also for others. Thomas Merton states that, "The stronger our love, the greater will be our ability to bear responsibility not only for ourselves but for others" (Merton 109). We encourage our readers to read works of Merton. As such, this researcher participated in a Benedictine Bible study for two years, with a local group in Bethlehem, Pennsylvania. She sought to find connections in the works of Thomas Merton, a Benedictine Trappist monk, and to perform action research case study, gathering qualitative research. The purpose of the project centers on the exegesis of texts by Maximilian Kolbe and Thomas Merton.

Upon a trip to Italy from January 1, 2018, to January 13, 2018, the author visited Benedictine monasteries in Rome, Florence, and Venice. She attended activities at St. Peter's in Rome. In Florence, she visited San Miniato, a Benedictine monastery. The monastery is San Miniato Al Monte, a splendid church overlooking one of the most beautiful and panoramic areas of Tuscany. Since that day, this researcher had had a faith renewal. She also gained a desire to share the knowledge that personal prayer and devotions that are contemplative in origin may connect us to God and may sustain the overall peaceful nature of human kindness. Cîteaux Abbey was founded on Saint Benedict's Day, 21 March 1098, by a group of monks from the abbey seeking to follow *The Rule of St. Benedict.* Merton is a Cistercian monk who follows the traditions of the first group of monks so long ago.

Interpreting short passages of the psalms awakens us to our own relationship with the presence of God. We interpret Psalm 23 by a literary analysis of one short passage: "The Lord is my Shepherd; I shall not want." Taking the focus on love from Kolbe and the focus on solitude by Merton, we reflect on Psalm 23 through the understanding of previous interpretations which mention that the Book of Psalms is the third section of the Hebrew Bible. Psalm 23 was used in worship by ancient Hebrews. The writer describes God as his shepherd. Currently, the psalm is recited and sung by Jews and Christians. It is a wonderful psalm about the universal theme of trusting God. Yet, key words give us a message of love. "I shall not want" reminds us of times when we did not have money to pay for needs. This personal view of the Bible allows us to reflect on our faith journey in a metacognitive mindfulness, to recall previous writing or experiences. Thoughtful analysis through reading and rereading and mindful meditative silence heal us. Sharing the materials and meditations that Kolbe wrote changed this researcher's heart toward suffering. Her father's suffering in a prison camp in World War II stayed within the memory of the researcher. She learned to be compassionate toward herself and her sadness. Therefore, prayer with the St. Kolbe manuscripts, such as his newsletter that she received, brought a focus on prayer that was extraordinary.

Twenty-five years ago, this researcher reflected on her interpretation of suffering; healing from illness may have been due to miracles which occurred after prayer and good works modeled upon the devotions to the Immaculata. Kolbe was born on January 8, 1894, in Zdunska-Wola, Poland. Dr. DiEdwardo's devotions began as a child when her father, who was Polish, often talked about Poland and Catholicism. In the journey of faith, we may reflect on our past to create writing about our current faith and healings from prayers and devotions. Currently, this researcher is Episcopal. She is volunteering in a soup kitchen at a local Episcopal church. Yet, as a devoted researcher of St. Kolbe, she promotes his writing and the history of World War II. To share the sadness and hope of the 20th century is to become a hermeneutic scholar. When the Nazis suppressed Kolbe's printing and publishing apostolate, his zeal remained steadfast. He forgave his enemies. On February 17, 1941, Father Maximilian Kolbe was arrested by the Nazis for a second time. Only hours before the Gestapo arrived, he completed his final and most comprehensive theological essay on the Virgin Mary's identity, as one who is perfectly united to the Holy Spirit by a bond of love. Soon after, in the concentration camp, Father Maximilian would translate his hopeful words for his fellow inmates. This researcher's father told stories about the time that he was a prisoner of war, held in Germany, and part of the Black March by the Nazis. Her father survived by eating tree roots. Looking back on the conversations with her father prove to this researcher that the study of history and the applications of hermeneutics are essential to try to emulate good people, people of God. With a focus on love, we acknowledge the importance of Marian devotions. Kolbe created a movement known as Marian-Franciscan. This researcher seeks to share the devotion to Kolbe's life and works. The time spent with the printed materials that were created by Kolbe has been evidence that exegesis of a text, such as literary analysis of the statement of Revelation: "Certainly, You alone and Your Mother are from every aspect completely beautiful. There is no blemish in You my Lord, and no stain in Your Mother" (Kolbe, "Brochure"). By directly speaking to the Lord, in the first person, "You," St. Kolbe continues to teach us. He also writes: "Let me be a fit instrument in your immaculate and merciful hands for introducing and increasing your glory to the maximum in all the many strayed and indifferent souls, and thus help extend as far as possible the blessed kingdom of the Most Sacred Heart of Jesus" (Kolbe, "Official Act"). We honor the language and literary structure of the words of St. Maximilian Kolbe. Through lexical-syntactical analysis, we note the importance of the words "blessed kingdom." For instance, the heart of Jesus's teaching centers on the kingdom of God. The expression is found sixty-one times in the Synoptic Gospels.

Works Cited

Grant, Robert M., David Tracy. *A Short History of the Interpretation of the Bible*, rev. ed. New York: Macmillan, 1963.

Kolbe, Maximilian. *Behold Your Mother*. "Militia of the Immaculata." Brochure, 2018.

---. *Official Act of Consecration to Mary*. "Militia of the Immaculata." Prayer Card, 2018.

Lipman, Matthew. "Critical thinking. What can it be?" *Educational Leadership*, 46, pp. 38–43.

Merton, Thomas. *Monastic Peace*. Abbey of Gethsemani, 1958.

---. Brother Patrick Hart, editor. *The Monastic Journey*. New York: Doubleday, 1978.

Ricoeur, Paul. *Hermeneutics*. Cambridge, UK: Polity Press, 2013.

The New Oxford Annotated Bible. Coogan, Michael D., et al., editors. New York: Oxford University Press, 2007, print.

Virkler, Henry A., and Karelynne Ayayo. *Hermeneutics: Principles and Processes of Biblical Interpretation, Second Edition*. 2007.

Chapter 3

Social Movements: Frank Bidart, Zora Neale Hurston, and Jack Kerouac

Dr. Maryann P. DiEdwardo

Lehigh University;
University of Maryland Global Campus

Social movements initiated by literature include The Beat Generation of the 1940s and 1950s, which questioned the existence of certain societal elements identified with Jack Kerouac, from a 1948 conversation with fellow Beat Poet and author John Clellon Holmes. Other social movements by luminaries such as Dietrich Bonhoeffer, Flannery O'Connor, Thomas Merton, and Martin Luther King Jr. ask us to reimagine literary works as social criticism: writers are agents of change. As such, we recognize the writing of Bonhoeffer, Merton, and M. L. King Jr. as well as the journaling of Flannery O'Connor as a daily writing practice paramount to a writer's ethic. But the powerful language and poetics of the work by Flannery O'Connor change us as we experience her inner life.

The poet Frank Bidart uses narrative strategies. His works of poetry embody the flow of human emotions. The pathos appeals to emotions and feelings, to persuade an audience. Bidart's dramatic monologues are an intrapersonal lens into the inner pain innate in the human emotional experience. Frank Bidart was born in Bakersfield, California, on May 27, 1939. His recent works include *Half-Light: Collected Poems 1965–2016*, published in 2017. This book won the National Book Award and the Pulitzer Prize. He is a messenger of hope for us. His writing is prophetic, motivational, and steadily charges forward with exceptional and theoretical foundations. One can see that the poet Frank Bidart uses mythological theory. He mindfully embraces situations of courage and despair in his conversational poetry. As part of the LGBTQIA community, Bidart inspires equality.

Therefore, through a student-directed pedagogical model, with the models of Kerouac, Hurston, and Bidart, my writing classes fuse into a learning community for reflection, discovery, and peer editing for student motivation and success. I actively engage writers who possess qualities of memory based on human everyday experiences, similar to those experiences within literary works they read. I play podcasts of sample student essays that show how students recall events or conditions based on the relationship of reading to memory. One of my students recalls her own beliefs in mercy killing and relates her heritage based on family and cultural beliefs in the right to life. Students use life story writing next to recounting experiences that may help them find a thesis. We write for a global, multiethnic, and ageless audience. Stories can indeed reach all readers. To write, we engage memories of readings, life experiences, and imagination. Accordingly, these three patterns compose voice on the written page. Writing is an essential life skill needed for human dignity.

This chapter explores the social movements that correspond to immigration writing rooted in imaginative and travel literature: The Beat Generation of Jack Kerouac, the Magic Realism of Zora Neale Hurston, the *Odyssey* Homeric epic, and the heroic epic by John R. R. Tolkien. I engage in qualitative research projects for the purpose of creating a peaceful mindfulness and writing of both Hurston and Kerouac and argues that these authors' works have roots in the nature of the Homeric epic *Odyssey*, which meditates on accepting the losses inflicted by life. Similarly, J. R. R. Tolkien of Oxford, England, translated four volumes by the renowned hobbits Bilbo and Frodo Baggins, written during the Third Age of Middle Earth, far longer ago than the Celtic, Germanic, and Icelandic manuscripts Professor Tolkien was used to deciphering. The result was *The Hobbit*. By applying hermeneutical approaches which emphasize the critique as a methodology, we intend to develop this study to include insights into Zora Neale Hurston, a visionary writer of African American culture of the 20th century, in the manner of creative thought.

We also see both writers, Hurston and Kerouac, as creators of immigration as a path to self-identity. The basis for literary thought is the *Odyssey* Homeric epic. Both writers find writing as a social function to reveal truths about the human condition through their immigration to places of culturally rich stories about important human actions. Casual inference refers to a manner of reasoning which permits an individual to see causal relationships in events and infer associations between and among them. These lead one to make conclusions (inferences) that are more likely to be true and justified.

To enhance my study, I compare Hurston's work to Jack Kerouac, who was born in the early 20th century. He authored *On the Road* and *The Subterraneans*. Freedom to immigrate to place defines human dignity because we seek agency and sociocultural signs. Kerouac witnesses Neal Cassady, and Hurston witnesses a zombie. Immigration to a different place offers the writer themes for new books to publish.

The poetics of Zora Neale Hurston, in her work *Tell My* Horse, tells us about deeply moving tales. She is a notable writer. To motivate writers of all ages, we have consistently written examples of pieces to inspire. In writing for global audiences and writers, from 1995 to the present, this author taught the methodology of Hurston and Kerouac: Experience by immigrating to other places with other people, then write. In 2008, when this author set out to design an enthralling and interesting literary study for Lehigh University Composition and Literature, she decided to teach Kerouac. In the past eight years, she has read all the work that Kerouac wrote, and recently she visited San Francisco, which regenerated a quest to understand and to use the works of Kerouac.

In 2019, this researcher's book, titled *Spacializing Social Justice: Literary Critiques*, was published; the research focused on discovering the importance of the writings of Zora Neale Hurston. The Zora Neale Hurston Digital Archive forms the basis of my essential argument that the works of Zora Neale Hurston invite continued research (Zora Neale Hurston Digital Archive). This researcher intends to design a study that relates Zora's writing to promote more critiques of her works. The study of hermeneutics of Zora Neale Hurston is a 21st-century phenomenon. This researcher has been listed in the Zora Neale Hurston Digital Archive. The 2016 research credit is for *American Women Writers, Poetics, and the Nature of Gender Study,* Maryann P. DiEdwardo, editor. The Chapter is about the use of place in fiction by Zora Neale Hurston and Stephanie Powell Watts. The researcher juxtaposes of post-structuralism and postmodern philosophical paradigms, participates in interdisciplinary theory and practice, and argues for literacy as the lifelong intellectual process of gaining meaning from a critical interpretation of written or printed text. Literary critiques explore the writer's mind as symbolic within the message of the words. Our poetics that generate the most healing are usually those coming from our inner core. Zora Neale Hurston was influenced in the 20th century by Nella Larsen. Both authors show us how to write about real events in order to make a difference. Nella Larsen is as imperative for 21st-century literary scholarship and in the same capacity as we include Langston Hughes. She offers us methodology and pedagogical structure, which allows writers to explore the period of the Harlem Renaissance within the themes of post feminism and the many ways in which women are often fearful and subject to rape and other kinds of violence. In her writing, Nella Larsen also examines the politically and economically underprivileged. Maryann examines the significance of the message of suffering in Willa Cather's *My Mortal Enemy*. Maryann DiEdwardo's original essay, "Semiotics, Connectivity, and Social Order of Imagined Architecture in Fiction Works" won the Karen Lentz Award in Denver at the 2016 Conferences College English Association for Adjunct or Contingent Faculty Presentation. Haitian folklore and the works of Zora Neale Hurston underlie important elements that still carry vital information. This researcher began to study Zora as a literary scholar when she was recognized by Alice Walker at the MLA convention in the 20th century. Zora Neale Hurston, novelist, folklorist, anthropologist, and ethnographer, was known during the Harlem Renaissance for her wit, irreverence, and folk writing style.

Hermeneutics forms the study of the literary imagination of Zora Neale Hurston. We center on observation of Hurston's writing as extraordinary in the areas of literary studies and cultural studies. Zora offers us an ethnographic view into the feminine as a spiritual quest. Stories are openings into the soul. Paradoxically, poetics which determine that the work speaks the truth. I seek to prove that Hurston reaches our souls to write. "She has two voices: her spiritual self and her ethnographic self" (Maryann P. DiEdwardo 11).

Zora Neale Hurston was born on Wednesday, January 7, 1891, in Notasulga, Alabama, and died on Thursday, January 28, 1960, in Fort Pierce, Florida, at the age of sixty-nine years. Hermeneutic evaluation of Hurston's story brings haunting appropriation of cultural significance of the writing of Hurston. It is the curious and the metaphysical originating from Plato that comes to us as life reflects the spiritual. Zora writes authentic expressions. Zora's text is connected to the themes of her writings during the period when she wrote the story. The hermeneutics of Zora Neale Hurston serve to recognize the mythic representation as the creator of openings into the soul. Imaginative literature often uses the spirituality of the author. Zora certainly used her powerful imaginative language to speak of cultural change. Through my own writing and imagination, I seek to prove that Hurston acts as a mirror into cultural changes necessary for all humanity.

Evaluation of Hurston's life brings a conceptual vision of space as literary creative process. "We find ourselves as passengers on journeys into the creative process of a great voice in the story by Hurston. She shows us how to be curious of all of life, even the harder parts to understand, death and representations of the dead human as a wailing creature, or zombie. It is the curious and the metaphysical originating from Plato that comes to us as life reflects the spiritual" (Maryann P. DiEdwardo 12).

Imaginative literature utilizes a reflection of reality. Writers and poets act as visionaries who compress emotions into words. "Mythical in theme, zombie archetypes offer visions of experiences beyond the human realm. Zombie archetypes of the masculine and feminine reverse roles and create death as a paradigm for healing from the pain of life on earth. We are a grieving culture. We are a spiritual culture. We are not alone. We can write based on past cultural milieu. We like to use memes to represent ourselves" (Maryann P. DiEdwardo 20).

Zombie archetypes may act as historically spiritual foundations. For me, as a creative nonfiction author, the zombie archetype is a myth in the form of spiritual awakening. The soul may be the connection between the story, the student, the poem, and the reflection of reality. Harmony may result by archetypal study of yin, feminine, and yang, masculine. We are now not past and not future. Encourage students to publish e-books in blogs, personal websites, WordPress, or as hard copies. Self-publishing is a method to encourage writers to succeed. Maryann P. DiEdwardo found her muse within the study of the works of Zora Neale Hurston. Maryann wrote a persona monologue that is called *The White Curtain*. It is published as an e-book.

Works Cited

Czech, Paul. Zora Neale Hurston Digital Archive, "Archive Manuscript Collection." chdr.cah.ucf.edu/hurstonarchive/?p=archive-collections. Accessed 3 Oct. 2019.

DiEdwardo, Maryann. *American Women Writers, Poetics, and the Nature of Gender Study.* England: Cambridge Scholars Publishing, 2017.

---. *Spatializing Social Justice: Literary Critiques.* New York: Hamilton Books, 2019.

Hurston, Zora Neale. *Tell My Horse: Voodoo and Life in Haiti and America.* New York: Harper, 1938.

Chapter 4

The Development and Impact of Joy Adamson's Work with Lions in Africa

Patricia J. Pasda, B.F.A., M.F.A.

Syracuse University

Joy Adamson first entered my life as my childhood hero. From the time my father brought me her books about Elsa, during grade-school years, I looked forward to living African adventures through Adamson's eyes. Arriving home from school, I would race to my literary treasures and vicariously live the life of the brave woman and Elsa, the orphaned cub, and her two sisters (Adamson 20–21). Loved and fiercely defended and cared for by Joy and her game warden–husband, George, in the wilds of Kenya, Elsa earned a permanent place in my heart.

I wasn't alone. The three novels, *Born Free: A Lioness of Two Worlds*, *Living Free: The Story of Elsa and Her Cubs*, and *Forever Free: Elsa's Pride*, were worldwide best-selling books and for all time changed the way conservationists viewed the lion species in the captive world of cages versus the way they were meant to live, in open spaces, or, as Joy so eloquently wrote, Elsa was "free born" (Adamson 220). The purpose of my research is to study the impact of Joy Adamson's work with lions in Africa and the effect of this work on current handling of conservation of this endangered species. Hermeneutics aids this researcher in the approach of collecting and analyzing data, allowing for the variables of human reasoning in collecting and understanding quantitative data (Mantzavinos).

Joy Adamson's innovative idea was to train her beloved friend and loved one, Elsa, to live the free life of a wild lion. Joy believed it was Elsa's rightful inheritance, and it started a chain of events that spawned many scientific studies, media presentations, and literary projects. Technology evolved and, as it continues to do so, the positive and negative points of hermeneutics affect the ever-lowering population of the African lion. The population of the African lion has decreased forty-two percent in the last twenty-one years (Platt).

Joy logged Elsa's story using environmental and naturalist study methods of the time. Accurate times and dates of Elsa's progress in growth and behavior ensued in Joy's journals and it became apparent that Elsa was the smaller and slower of the three cubs. These facts and the motherly instincts that developed in Joy with the relationship between Joy and Elsa formed the basis for the bond that would enable the two to survive the struggle ahead, and help Elsa to learn to live as a lioness in the wild. In the first part of their existence, the cubs actually lived in the house with the Adamsons, free to roam and play, watched over by Joy's pet hyrax Patty (Adamson 10).

George provided fresh meat, so once the cubs were weaned off milk, they began eating the proper diet of a true carnivore. Elsa's sisters grew larger and stronger and Elsa also grew and eventually all three had to move outside the Adamsons' home. Moreover, the local authorities demanded that the lions be moved to a zoo since they were unafraid of humans. Joy and George complied— with Elsa's sisters. When it came to Elsa, Joy refused to put her in a cage, saying that she was "free born" and that was how she should live. Joy fought for Elsa to have her chance at freedom, like she had fought for her own freedom. Joy had found her own freedom in Africa; so too would Elsa.

The authorities gave the Adamsons a chance to try. Joy, George, and Elsa faced many challenges. Elsa needed to learn how to hunt and feed herself safely, and how to approach a water hole filled with hippos and crocodiles and lined with water buffalo. Other dangers, like stampeding antelope or brush fires, angry baboons and rival lionesses, threatened her survival in the wild. The family started close to their home, and after Elsa had most skills down, many months had passed. Her first experience living with wild lions proved difficult and she returned, sickly, injured, and starved, to Joy and George, prompting George to plead with Joy to send her to the zoo with her sisters. Joy fought again for Elsa's right to live as she was born … free and in the wild.

Their next strategy sent the three to another area, which brought success. Months passed, and a male lion accepted Elsa. She joined him and lived free. Hard as it was, Joy left her beloved Elsa and returned to her home camp, later known as Elsamere. She continued to write her book *Born Free*, even traveling to England and back for publishing obligations.

George still worked as a game warden and of course, checked on Elsa. Joy's return brought emotional visits, when Elsa would control her great strength in her hugs and greetings so as not to injure Joy. A postscript to the book *Born Free* explains that Elsa's cubs were born. Miraculously, when they were strong enough, Elsa brought along her three cubs to meet her human family.

Careful not to handle the young ones, Joy still hugged her dear Elsa like when Elsa greeted her human mom in her traditional fashion.

The cubs grew within their small pride and things proceeded naturally, until Elsa contracted babesiosis, a blood-borne illness from insects. At age five, she died in George's arms when Joy was traveling. The male lion left his cubs in the hands of Joy and George, apparently wandering off. Since lions mature over the course of approximately three years, Joy once again faced the even greater challenge of finding a home free of poachers, and protected, for Elsa's offspring to live free.

Ultimately the Serengeti National Park became Jespah, Gopa, and Little Elsa's home. They remained as wild as possible and they could identify Joy and George by scent and sight (Adamson 161).

Joy wrote many books and helped other species, including cheetahs (Adamson) and started the Elsa Wild Animal Appeal to help preserve the area where Elsa's grave exists and where the cubs lived at the time. Upon Joy Adamson's death, more heroes of conservation emerged related to Elsa and Joy. Virginia McKenna and Bill Travers, the actress and actor who had played Joy and George in the feature film *Born Free*, based on Joy's book, founded the Born Free Foundation, an international charity organization. This organization is worldwide and places animals held in captivity back in the wild, in great numbers, under protective care, and is represented in many countries. George Adamson continued their mission until his death and the Born Free Foundation also continues all of George's work, including the Meru National Park where Christian the lion was released (Bourke 25), and where Elsa's grave is preserved.

Today, Elsa's descendants thrive in the Meru Reserve and are protected and studied by the Born Free Foundation and other wildlife conservation organizations.

People may think of flora and fauna and their relationship to the cultural milieu of a nation as a science, but in reality, the social mores of a society and humanitarian efforts determine the survival of species in the wild. Moreover, how exotic species are handled in a society, in social situations, can injure a species and become the catalyst for organizations such as the Born Free Foundation, which calls on humanity the world over to police the masses for animals held in captivity that are inappropriately treated, such as the case of the tiny young lion King, found in a Paris apartment. His story is my story, for his plight compelled me to help in his adoption, start a fundraiser on social media to help him, and I continue to follow the story of his life. Thanks to thousands of people throughout the world, led by Virginia McKenna, trustee and founder of the Born Free Foundation, King was taken from the substandard, abusive situation and brought back to health. Filmed for the world to see, with the Born Free Center manager Katherine Gillson guiding us, King was released in the Shamwari Cape of South Africa, where he will grow in the protected area of the Born Free Foundation Lion Reserve, safe from poachers and hunters (Born Free Foundation, *King's Story, Journey to Africa* video).

Yes, Joy Adamson's work with lions in Africa began with her determination that the lioness, Elsa, which she raised and loved, who was born free, would live free. Today there are millions of us connected by social media, traditional mail, radio broadcasts, and any connection we can make, all determined to help the species of the African lion and countless others avoid extinction. The science of species survival has become for us, as humans, a social science where we reach out to one another so that our planet and our animals may live. Joy's legacy lives in the Born Free Foundation and other organizations like it. In the United States, the University of Minnesota has a significant program concerning the protection of lions in Kenya.

Joy's message of hope that lions and other animals meant for life in the wild will live their lives free in their inheritance depends on people like us continuing to share the written works of authors like Joy Adamson and making this information available on the social media of the day. Proof of the impact Joy Adamson's work with lions in Africa exists is clearly found in social media and thrives in rescued lions like King and in Elsa's pride on the plains of the Meru Reserve (Born Free Foundation).

Understanding the social structure and development of this big cat's life, compiled with the influence of a pride's impact on the surrounding species in a given area, prompts environmental programs and groups to repopulate the African lion where more success rates are possible.

A varying degree of success in protecting the existence of lions in the wild in protective custodial areas or preserves in South Africa and Kenya is most likely to continue at the time of this writing. The topic of my research concerning Joy Adamson grew into a volume highlighting the very essence of hermeneutics, noting that Elsa is a parallel to Joy's own life as a survivor of the Nazi occupation of Austria.

Joy's mysterious past and the current release of the knowledge that she is indeed An Austrian Jewish refugee from World War Two who found freedom in Africa reflects strongly on her view of freedom.

Joy became emotionally attached to the lion cub Elsa due to Elsa's being the weaker cub who fought harder for life itself. As Elsa grew older and her sisters were transferred to a London zoo, I feel Joy related her own her fight—for the freedom she found in Africa—to Elsa and worked hard to help the growing lioness find freedom as a lion in Africa. Joy's words are usually quoted as "but she was free born," which I see as an autobiographical statement from her own heart (Adamson 220).

Applying human emotion in kind to animals is part of hermeneutics and the new hermeneutics wave in naturalism and in studying animals in the wild or as part of scientific study in hermeneutic philosophy (Platt).

Therefore, in the hermeneutics approach, the cause of Joy's success with Elsa's freedom was Joy's firm belief in Elsa's right to live free, and this snowballed through each person exposed to Joy's work, into the great conservation effort we have and desperately need to keep vibrant today. Nearly five hundred of Joy Adamson's paintings are preserved and on display in the Joy Adamson Museum in Nairobi, Kenya, for she is the recognized mother of African conservation.

Works Cited

Adamson, Joy. *Born Free: A Lioness of Two Worlds*. Pantheon, 1960.

---. *Living Free*. New York: Harcourt, 1961.

Born Free. www.bornfree.org.uk. Accessed 3 Oct. 2019.

Born Free Foundation. *King's Story, Journey to Africa* video. www.youtube.com/watch?v=DOSMUQltRY4. Accessed 23 July 2018.

Bourke, Anthony and John Rendall. *A Lion Called Christian*. Broadway Books, 1971.

Mantzavinos, C. "Hermeneutics." Standford Encyclopedia of Philosophy. plato.stanford.edu/entries/hermeneutics/. Accessed Jan. 2019.

Platt, John R. "Extinction Count Down. African Lion Population Drop 42 Percent in Past 21 Years." Scientific America Blog. blogs.scientificamerican.com/extinction-countdown/african-lion-populations-drop-42-percent-in-past-21-years/. Accessed Sept. 2019.

**THE ELSA
WILD ANIMAL APPEAL**

Donations: c/o CHARITIES AID FUND, 48 Pembury Road, Tonbridge, Kent, Tonbridge 62823.
Registered Office: 34 South Molton Street, London W.1, 01 - 629 - 9871
Administration: The Secretary, Mrs. J.E. AUCUTT, The Elsa Wild Animal Appeal, London W1A 4XL, 01 - 289 - 2820.

Your Ref.
Our Ref.

Dear Patti:

      Thank you very much for your kind letter. I am
glad to know that you like my books about "Elsa" and
"Pippa" and that you take so much interest in their
fate. Unfortunately we have never found Elsa's cubs
despite the fact that we searched for 19 months for
them. With Pippa's offspring I was more lucky and on
my frequent visits to the Meru National Park saw two
of her daughters already with their own cubs, totalling
seven. Since cheetah do not breed well in captivity
and decline alarmingly in nature, I am especially happy
to have found a way of successfully breeding them under
natural conditions and thus can save these magnificent
cats from becoming extinct.

      Additional to these books on lion and cheetah I
have written THE PEOPLES OF KENYA in which I describe
the traditional customs of the Africans before foreign
contact influenced their lives. My latest book is
called JOY ADAMSON'S AFRICA showing some of my
paintings with descriptive text.

      Now we are launching a one hour weekly TV series
for NBC, based on Elsa and Born Free, which will
follow the concept and philosophy of the work we have
done in the past. We expect this series to be on the
air in September 1974.

      All the royalties I obtain from my books and
the films are used for the benefit of wild animals.
However large this sum may be, it will not suffice to
cover even their most urgent needs. Should you or
your friends care to help, we would be most grateful
for your co-operation in our work as well as for
donations to the "Elsa Wild Animal Appeal". All
contributions are exempt from tax and should be sent
to the following addresses:

ENGLAND   U.S.A.

The Elsa Wild Animal Appeal,   The Elsa Wild Animal
c/o The Charities Aid Fund,   Appeal,
48 Pembury Road,   P.O. Box 4572,
Tonbridge, KENT.   North Hollywood,
                                     CALIFORNIA 91607.

CANADA   KENYA

The Elsa Wild Animal Appeal   The Elsa Wild Animal
                of Canada,   Appeal,
P.O. Box 864,   c/o Livingstone
Postal Station 'K',   Registrars Limited,
Toronto 12, ONTARIO   P.O. Box 30029, NAIROBI

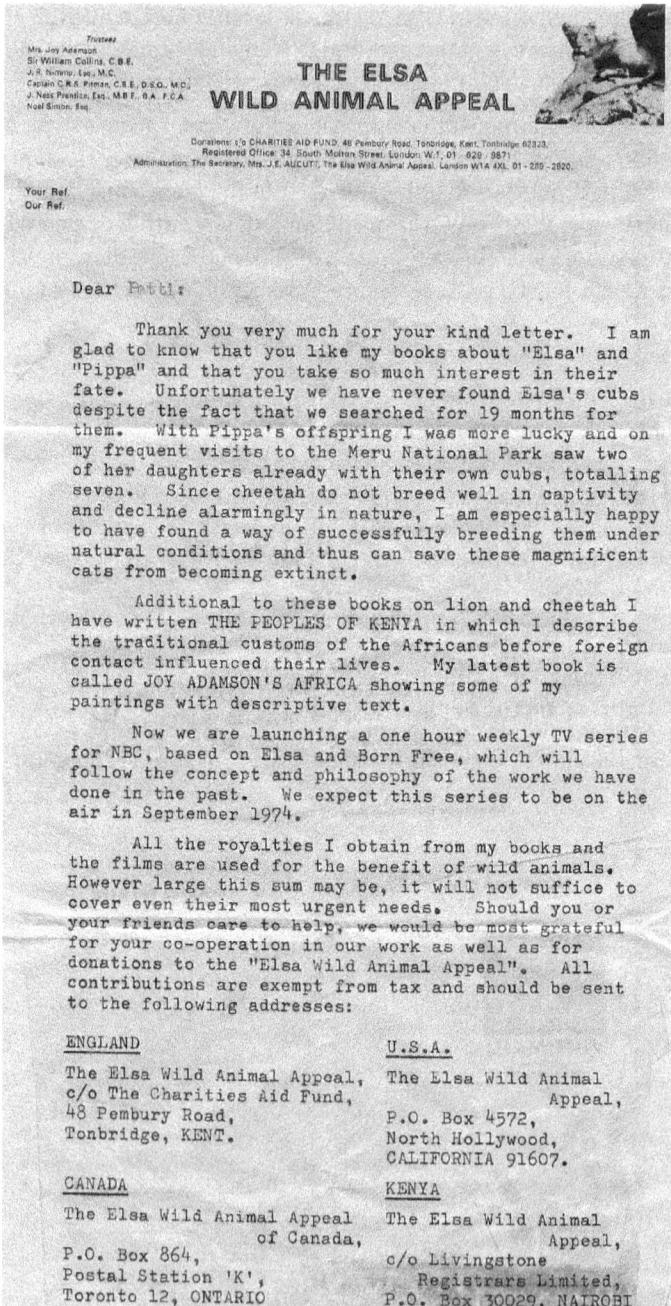

Figure 2. Letter from Joy Adamson to the author Patricia Pasda, B.F.A., M.F.A.

P.S. I was very touched by your letter and sorry that I have no
time to write a longer personal letter. As to your inquiries, I
have been averaging twice a year to Meru National Park and only
returned from my last visit yesterday and found two of Pippa's
cubs, each have a litter totaling 10 cubs. I will endeavor to
find on future visits more out about them especially as I have
never found her last litter described in "Pippa's Challenge".
As far as today's necessary education for any work dealing with
domestic or wild animals, you would have to have a veterinarian
or zoological degree. It is impossible to get in Kenya a paid
job unless you get a work permit which costs £100, which is almost impossible to get for a non-citizen, and even then, Africans
have priority. You are quite right that we can learn tremendously
from animals who solve our mutual problems often far more cleverly
than we humans do, for example in birth control.
Thank you again for writing.

Yours sincerely

Joy Adamson

FIRST FOLD HERE   KUNJO LA KWANZA HAPA

Sender's name and address:

AN AIR LETTER SHOULD NOT CONTAIN ANY
ENCLOSURE; IF IT DOES IT WILL BE SURCHARGED
OR SENT BY ORDINARY MAIL.

Issued by the East African Posts and Telecommunications Corporation

SECOND FOLD HERE   KUNJO LA PILI HAPA

AIR MAIL
PAR AVION
AEROGRAMME

KENYA
TANZANIA
UGANDA
70c

Miss Patti Pasda

1940 Dartmouth Drive

Figure 3. Letter from Joy Adamson to the author Patricia Pasda, B.F.A., M.F.A.

Chapter 5

"Mrs. Hitchcock's Coming Out Party: The Injustice to Women in Hitchcock's Life Revealed in Films"

Dr. T. Madison Peschock

Ocean County College

For the last five decades, Alfred Hitchcock has been known as a cult icon. He is considered the Master of Suspense, and often referred to as one of the greatest directors of all time. With such classics as: *Dial M for Murder* (1954), *Rear Window* (1954), *Vertigo* (1958), *North by Northwest* (1959), *Psycho* (1960), *The Birds* (1963), and *Alfred Hitchcock Presents* TV show (1955–1962), Hitchcock had millions of fans worldwide, and at the time of his death in 1980, he was praised at "among the greatest artists of this century" (Miller). However, in 1983, with the publication of Donald Spoto's biography, *The Dark Side of Genius*, Hitchcock's reputation took a hit when Spoto revealed that the famed director sexually harassed actress Tippi Hedren on the sets of *The Birds* and *Marnie*. Those who paid close attention to book reviews or read the biography would have discovered this information, but did they believe it or even care in 1983? Was Hedren lying for attention or trying to get back at Hitchcock for something? At that time, not much was made of Hedren's claims. However, jump ahead to 2012 and times have changed. Not only has Hedren released her own autobiography, *Tippi: A Memoir*, in which she discusses the harassment at great lengths, but there is also a biopic, *The Girl* which focusses entirely on Hedren's claims of harassment and abuse. That same year, a second film, *Hitchcock*, was released that also reveals Hitchcock's wife's role in his work. For years, Alma Reville Hitchcock was the great woman behind the man who did not receive the proper credit she should have. Thus, with the release of these two biopics about Hitchcock's life, is Hitchcock's reputation still that of a great director? After watching two 2012 biopics about the director's life, it appears that Hitchcock made a career out of using women to advance his own career; therefore, we need to reevaluate our views about the director. His legacy should be one that includes his injustices towards women, and by reevaluating

Hitchcock's legacy, students and faculty of film, literature and composition will have great topics to write about and discuss.

When Alfred Hitchcock died in 1980, many thought of him as a directorial genius. According to James Steward, "I have never worked with anyone who was more considerate, more helpful, more understanding of actors that Hitchcock" (Miller). But in 1983, Tippi Hedren did not feel that way and was the first actress to discuss her negative experiences working with Hitchcock when she shared with Donald Spoto how he traumatized her and sexually harassed her while working on *The Birds* and *Marnie.* Well before the #Me Too movement that began in 2017, Tippi Hedren, like many women who have been sexually harassed, waited decades to come forward and share her painful stories publically about how Hitchcock treated her. It is because of Hedren's bravery that the world now can understand who the real Alfred Hitchcock was, which is portrayed in HBO's *The Girl.*

Set from 1961–1964 during Hitchcock's work on *The Birds* and *Marnie, The Girl* explores the famed director's relationship with actress Tippi Hedren (Sienna Miller) and shows Hitchcock's (Toby Jones) growing obsession with her and his eventual physical and mental abuse of her. While the film's primary goal is to tell the story of how Hitchcock supposedly ruined Hedren's career, the film also reveals Hitchcock's relationship with his wife, Alma (Imelda Staunton), and alludes to the fact that Hitch and Alma had a loveless marriage. Furthermore, the film suggests that Alma was involved in helping Hitchcock in his career, but shows that she was both a victim of Hitchcock's love for other women and an enabler of his abuse towards Hedren because she knew of his obsession for her and did not put a stop to it.

The Girl is based on Donald Spoto's *The Dark Side of Genius: The Life of Alfred Hitchcock*, and is Hedren's account of what happened. The film, written by Gwyneth Hughes, also "was based on conversations with surviving members of Hitchcock's crew" (Rampton). Of course, there are those who believe Hedren and others, such as Norman Lloyd, a star in two of Hitchcock's films, who do not. This is because Hedren waited decades to come forward to tell her story and did not do so until 1983, when Hitchcock had already been dead three years.

The Girl begins with Hitchcock searching for a new actress to star in his new project, *The Birds*, and shows Hitchcock eating with his wife, while *SHE* points out a new, young blonde to him. Thus, it is his wife who spots Hedren in a diet drink commercial for Sego (Spoto, *Darkside* 449). Immediately, Hitchcock has his people contact "THE GIRL" (Hedren) who has not acted in any films prior to meeting him. Hedren (Sienna Miller) meets the famed director for an introductory meeting and then a screen test, in which his wife, Alma, is present. After Alma approves of Hedren, Hitchcock signs her to a seven-year contract, which she excitedly accepts, saying, "I'll make you so proud of me. I'll be putty in your hands" (*The Girl*). At this point, Hedren does not realize what is about to occur during the next few years.

The remainder of the film concentrates on Hitchcock's obsessive and abusiveness relationship towards Hedren. For instance, while filming *The Birds*, in the back of his Rolls Royce, while on a ride back from Bodega Bay, where parts of *The Birds* was filmed, Hitchcock forces himself on her. He touches her leg and breast and kisses her passionately as she desperately tries to get him to stop by pushing him away. As the car pulls up to the studio, Hedren runs from it as the film crew looks at her with uncertainty. Hedren confirmed this story to Donald Spoto, which he writes about in *Spellbound by Beauty: Hitchcock and His Leading Ladies*. Hedren stated, "I pushed him away and got out of the car, and I thought I would give him the benefit of the doubt—maybe he was just trying to make me nervous," but the abuse persisted (253). Hedren writes in her own autobiography, "It was an awful, awful moment I'll always wish I could erase from my memory. The next time I saw him was on the set. I dreaded seeing him again, but I wasn't about to give him the satisfaction of knowing how deeply he'd offended and affected me" (Hedren 51).

After the car incident, Hitchcock is seen continually spouting dirty limericks in front of Hedren, and he tries to touch her every chance he gets. According to actress Sienna Miller, who had met and spoken extensively to Tippi Hedren to prepare for her role, Hedren told her, "he even told [me] what lipstick to wear" (Rampton). However, the worst abuse is when Hedren filmed the final scene of *The Birds* known as the attic scene. Hedren was told by both producers and Hitchcock that the shoot would take one day and that they would use mechanical birds that would attack her. Instead, she was subjected to 45 takes over five days of shooting with live birds (Spoto, *Spellbound* 187). Actor, Rod Taylor recalls, "Men stood Tippi in the corner ... and just began throwing birds at her ... one after another; again and again, take after take" (255). After the attic scene, the film shows Hedren's mental breakdown and need for time off from filming because of Hitchcock's abuse. In one scene, she tells her friend, Joanne, "There's no way he made up his mind that morning to use real birds. He knew they were going to use real birds. Stuff like that takes weeks to organize. He knew and he never told me" (*The Girl*). This too is true. According to biographer Donald Spoto, Hitchcock did not tell Hedren about the live birds. Instead, Assistant Director James Brown told her (*Spellbound* 458). However, what one takes away from watching *The Girl*, reading published articles about Hedren, and reading her autobiography is that filming the attic scene with live birds is Hedren's punishment for not accepting Hitchcock's sexual advances. According to Hedren, "He inflicted deep psychological damage on [me]" (Rampton). In another interview, Hedren said, "he ruined my career, but he didn't ruin my life" (Associated Press).

The second major point *The Girl* makes is that Hitchcock's wife knew of his sexual obsession with Hedren and other blonde actresses, and she never stopped it. First, the film shows how Mrs. Hitchcock knew of his love for blonde actresses. In one brief scene, Alma Hitchcock asks her husband's secretary, "Grace was pretty, Ingrid was pretty. What's this one got that's so special?" (*The Girl*). In another scene, Hitchcock states when discussing his wife, "I'm lost without her" (*The Girl*). While *The Girl* reveals Alma to be her husband's stabilizer, the film shows the lack of love the Hitchcock's had in their marriage. In one scene Hitchcock tells Hedren on the phone that "Alma's more like a sister to me. I only married her because she asked me to" (*The Girl*). But perhaps the biggest shock of the film is that Alma knew of her husband's harassment toward Hedren. This is seen when Alma approaches Hedren after her time on the set of *Marnie* and says to her, "I'm sorry you're having to go through this" (*The Girl*). Hedren responds by saying, "You could stop it. You're the only one who could stop it with one word, Alma, please" (*The Girl*). However, Mrs. Hitchcock just stares at Hedren and walks away. In a 2012 interview, Hedren, said, referring to Mrs. Hitchcock, "'She knew full well what was going on [...] 'It is a true and accurate story that needed to be told,'" (Oglethorpe). Hedren states in her own autobiography, "Alma had an enormous, well-deserved influence of her husband" (39). Furthermore, according to Hitchcock's daughter, Patricia, her mother ruled Hitchcock. Her opinion and word was final on all matters: she "was the most important person to him in anything" (O'Connell & Bouzereau 182). In fact, "Her word was absolute command" (183). *The Girl*, definitely gives this impression particularly when Hedren pleads with Alma for her to put a stop to her husband's philandering. According to Donald Spoto, Hedren "was hurt and surprised that Alma did not intervene … on her behalf" (*Spellbound* 274).

After *The Birds* was finished being filmed, Hitchcock's obsession with Hedren continued and worsened. According to Donald Spoto, "Jay Allen saw Hitchcock's treatment of Tippi, but she, too, was new to Hollywood and said nothing" (Spoto, *Spellbound* 263). According to Allen, "He was mad for her, just as he had been obsessed with a series of [...] blond[e] actresses before" (263). In *The Girl*, this obsession is seen as Hitchcock showers Hedren with presents, spies on her and even stalks her by having his chauffer drive him past her house. Worse yet, Hitchcock refuses to let Hedren out of her contract when she requested. In one of the film's most provocative scenes, Hitchcock tells Hedren, "From now on I want you to make yourself sexually available to me at all times. Whatever I want you to do whenever I want you to do it. Because I think that's only fair given what I've done for you" (*The Girl*). Immediately, Hedren responds, "NO; I want out of my contract" (*The Girl*). To this, Hitchcock threatens that he will ruin her career. He says, "Well you can't get out of it, can you? No one will hire you. What about your child, your parents in Minnesota? Tippi Hedren didn't have it. Alfred Hitchcock did his best but she just didn't have it. Her career went nowhere after she parted from the man who gave her everything" (*The Girl*). While this scene is one of the film's best, no sources except Hedren herself, have confirmed that these conversations actually occurred. She claimed in a recent interview when referring to *The Girl*, "It's a true depiction … the writer, Gwyneth Hughes worked with me on the script … or I should say, the other way around. It's the way I wanted it" ("Tippi Hedren interviewed by the Chiligods, Part 1"). However, did Mrs. Hitchcock know about this? No one seems to know. However, the surprising aspect of *The Girl* is that it reveals Hitchcock's own relationship with his wife, Alma.

While *The Girl* focuses primarily on Hitchcock's relationship with Hedren, dialogue and brief scenes allude to the fact that Alma Hitchcock was her husband's stabilizing force, and that the two worked together on Hitchcock's films. For instance, in one scene, Hitch and Alma are sitting in a screening room together watching a rough cut of *Marnie*. Alma says to her husband, "I'm not sure about the kiss. I was thinking I could go back to the set and work. You could use the support, especially on this scene, and I could use the entertainment" (*The Girl*). Although Alma is heard saying that she works with Hitchcock, there are no scenes that portray her working beside him or showing her importance to his career. What is revealed is that she knew and disapproved of his love for blondes.

Ultimately, the film ends by showing Hedren's relief about finishing *Marnie*, and never having to work with Hitchcock again. According to Hedren, he did ruin her career. In an interview, she stated, "I had to get out of there. […] I was dealing with one of the most powerful men in motion pictures and it was difficult, embarrassing and insulting. He said, 'If you leave, I'll ruin your career.' And he did" (Hiscock). Hedren said in a 2012 interview, I "would have been a rich woman if sexual harassment laws existed in 1963" (Malm). Thus, *The Girl* is an important film for showing Hedren's side of the matter and showing a workplace atmosphere in which "a powerful man's transgressions are ignored and enabled by the employees around him, all grateful passengers on the gravy train he is driving" (Doherty 6).

The same year as the release of *The Girl* in 2012, Fox Search Light's *Hitchcock* was released, but this film takes a more direct approach to showing Alma's contributions to her husband's career while he was working on *Psycho* in 1959. While the film centers on how *Psycho* was made, it concentrates heavily on Alma's involvement in the entire production. Throughout the film, Alma (Helen Mirren) not only shows her constant support of her husband's work, but Hitchcock is seen needing both her approval and her help as she is seen working alongside him in several scenes. Thus, the film finally gives Alma Reville Hitchcock credit publicly for helping her husband's career—an idea not known by many unless they read Pat Hitchcock's 2003 book, *Alma Hitchcock: The Woman Behind the Man.*

At the beginning of *Hitchcock*, both Hitchcock (Anthony Hopkins) and his wife are seen attending the premier of his latest successful film, *North by Northwest* in July 1959. The scene shows the couple walking hand-in-hand into the premiere as Alma purposely slips behind her husband so that he can take center stage to be interviewed by the press. This is the film's first clue that Alma was modest and knew her role in her husband's career. At this point in his life, the fame director is sixty years old and has directed "forty-six feature films and [had] three successful seasons [of *Alfred Hitchcock Presents*] on television" (Rebello 16). After the premiere, Hitchcock finds himself looking for his latest movie project, until he discovers Robert Bloch's novel, *Psycho*, based on Ed Gein and his murders in Plainfield, Wisconsin. Once Hitchcock decides to make *Psycho* the subject of his next film, his first action is to show the book to Alma.

In one of *Hitchcock*'s early scenes, Hitchcock is seen waking up Alma and asking her to read a section of Block's novel. Alma reads, "Mary started to scream, and then the curtains parted farther and a hand appeared holding a butcher's knife. It was the knife that a moment later cut off her scream and then her head" (*Hitchcock*). Sarcastically, Alma says, "charming! Doris Day should do it as a musical. This is nothing but low budget horror movie claptrap" (*Hitchcock*). Audiences can see Alma's disapproval of her husband's next project. The next morning, Hitchcock is still trying to persuade Alma to do *Psycho*. He says, "You are intrigued aren't you—killing off your leading lady half way though" (*Hitchcock*). Alma responds, "Actually, I think it's a huge mistake! You shouldn't wait till half way though, kill her off after 30 minutes" (*Hitchcock*). From this dialogue, it is clear that Alma has finally approved of *Psycho* as her husband's next picture. The film unfortunately gets this event incorrect. While it is true that Alma gave her full support for her husband to make *Psycho*, it was not until she read Joseph Stefano's opening scene in his screenplay. According to Hitchcock, "Alma loved it" (Rebello 43). Furthermore, according to Hitchcock's daughter, "When my mother did not like a script, my father would immediately abandon the idea. He always paid careful attention to what his wife had to say about his pictures" (O'Connell and Bouzereau 2). In fact, Alma "advised him on script material, casting and all aspects of production. Frequently, she co-wrote the screenplays and stood discreetly at his side during the production, in the editing room, and at the launching of each picture" (2). *Hitchcock* portrays many of these ideas.

Although Alma finally approved of *Psycho*, there were bigger problems because the studio would not let Hitchcock do the picture due to its violence and subject matter. If Hitchcock wanted to continue, he would have to finance the film himself. In *Hitchcock*, Hitch breaks the news to Alma, saying, "Paramount refuses to finance the movie. We'll just have to go it alone old girl and finance it ourselves" (*Hitchcock*). To this, Alma responds by asking, "so are we gonna have to sell the whole house or just the pool?" (*Hitchcock*). The film then takes the opportunity to display a tender moment between husband and wife that reveals the fact that the two worked together previously. During this scene, Hitchcock tears up and asks Alma:

> Do you remember the fun we had when we started out all those years ago? We didn't have any money then did we? We didn't have any time either, but we took risks. Do you remember? We experimented. We invented new ways of making pictures because we had to. I just want to feel that kind of freedom again like we used to ya know. (*Hitchcock*)

From this speech, it is clear to audiences that the husband and wife have worked together before, but exactly what films they have done together are never revealed. The truth, however, is that Alma Reville had an impressive film career. She worked as an assistant director, a screenwriter, editor, continuum girl, and film cutter. In fact, "When Hitchcock and Alma met, she was in the film business three or four years prior than him. Reville even was Hitchcock's boss briefly, but by 1923, he was beginning his directing career and hired her as his assistant" (Lowman). Because the film does not elaborate on Alma's exact contributions to Hitchcock's many films, audiences are left to wonder exactly what kind of film career Reville had. However, thanks to her daughter's book, *Alma Hitchcock: The Woman Behind The Man*, it is revealed that Reville had a long, successful career in cinema. In fact, Alma "was credited on nineteen out of fifty-three Hitchcock films, although it is sometimes thought that she was involved, however tangentially, in the production of every one" (Spoto, *Spellbound by Beauty* 86).

It is near the end of *Hitchcock* that Alma's most important contributions to *Psycho* are finally revealed when she is seen performing two important roles on the project. First, she assists her husband edit the film. However, Alma doe more than just edit because it is she who "spotted a glitch that her husband [and many other editors] had missed; Janet Leigh staring in fixed-eyed close up on the bathroom floor, gulped when she was supposed to have been dead" (Rebello 118). *Hitchcock* shows this idea when Alma and her husband are cutting *Psycho* together. Alma states, "You'll have to cut this six or seven frames; she blinks when she's supposed to be dead" (*Hitchcock*). Hitchcock responds, "Alma, we've viewed it hundreds of times; she does not blink" (*Hitchcock*). However, Alma simply smiles at Hitch and he knows she's correct, especially since he told her in the previous scene that "nobody knows how to cut a picture better than you my dear" (*Hitchcock*). While the film finally gives credit to Alma for her keen editing talents, the film distorts one specific. Janet Leigh gulped, not blinked. This is the first important contribution Alma makes to *Psycho* by showing her keen eye for editing. The second one is when she convinces her husband to use the violin score in the famous shower scene. Originally, Hitchcock "did not want Bernard Hermann's music in that scene, and Alma insisted. And it was only because of his absolute trust in her that it's included (Anderson). According to Nisha Lilia Diu, "Alma persuaded Hitchcock to listen to what Hermann was doing with that sequence, not just to reject it out of hand. [...] She really had a major impact on the film by just persuading Hitchcock to back off from his own ego and listen to the idea of somebody else" (Diu).

By the end of *Hitchcock*, viewers see a film that reveals how Alma is the stabilizing force in her husband's personal life by organizing his schedule, taking care of their finances, cooking his meals, but most importantly, her career in cinema and her role in her husband's career is finally made public—a fact that not many people have known about. In fact, Alma's role in Hitchcock's career was kept under wraps until 1979 when Hitchcock was honored by the American Film Institute for a lifetime achievement award. In his acceptance speech, Hitchcock said:

> I beg permission to mention by name only four people who have given me the most affection, appreciation, encouragement, and constant collaboration. The first of the fourth is a film editor, the second is a script writer, the third is the mother of my daughter, Pat, and the fourth is as fine a cook as ever performed miracles in a domestic kitchen, and their names are Alma Reville. Had the beautiful Miss Reville not accepted a lifetime contract, without options, as Mrs. Alfred Hitchcock some fifty-three years ago, Mr. Alfred Hitchcock might not be in the room tonight—not at this table but as one of the slow waiters on the floor. I share this award, as I have my life with Alma.
> (O'Connell & Bouzereau 220–221)

Hitchcock ends by making mention of this speech. Clearly, Hitchcock acknowledged his wife in public, but years after her contributions were already made, and how many people heard this speech? According to Nisha Lilia Diu, "Few beyond film historians and the notoriously tight-knit Hitchcock inner circle are aware of Mrs. Hitchcock's role in his 50-year career" (Diu). He once said with reference to his wife:

> It isn't my fault, really, that Alma has stayed so much out of sight of the public, although I suspect I'm accused a lot of overshadowing her. She does read for me and I rely on her opinion. [...] She's always on the set

the first day we begin shooting a film, … and always gives me her criticisms. (O'Connell & Bouzereau 174*)*

So, the question remains, why were Alma Reville's talents not celebrated more before these two films? Was it because no one cared? Was it because Hitchcock's daughter's book was published and this information was beginning to become known? Was it because the times were changing and women were finally beginning to receive long-overdue credit? No matter what the answer, both films give Reville her long-overdue praise and give voice to her contributions in her husband's works, a fact that has been unknown by the general public for far too long. *The Girl* is successful for bringing Tippi Hedren's complaints about Hitchcock to light to a larger audience. Perhaps this is what is to be gained by watching these two films—the injustice done to women. This topic—injustice to women—certainly gives film students, composition students, and literary students a chance to research the past, write about the present, and connect the two ideas. It is this topic—injustice—that allows students and faculty to hold conversations in the classroom, create assignments, and write about a topic that has become so common place for all. Thanks to these exceptional films, students and faculty will have plenty of writing and discussions to come, and finally, Alfred Hitchcock's true legacy can be understood.

Works Cited

Anderson, John. "Alfred Hitchcock's Secret Weapon Becomes a Star: 'Hitchcock' and 'The Girl' Remember Alma Reville." *The New York Times*. 16 Nov. 2012. www.nytimes.com/2012/11/18/movies/hitchcock-and-the-girl-remember-alma-reville.html. Accessed 1 Mar. 2013.

Associated Press. "Tippi Hedren Says Hitchcock Ruined her Career, Not her Life." *Daily Herald*. 4 Aug. 2012. www.dailyherald.com. 17 Feb. 2019.

Bidisha. "What's Wrong with Hitchcock's Women." *The Guardian*. 21 Oct. 2010. www.theguardian.com/film/2010/oct/21/alfred-hitchcock-women-psycho-the-birds-bidisha. Accessed 20 Jan. 2019.

Diu, Nish Lilia. "Mrs. Alfred Hitchcock: 'The Unsung Partner.' " The Telegraph. 8 Feb. 2013. www.telegraph.co.uk/culture/film/film-news/9832084/Mrs-Alfred-Hitchcock-The-Unsung-Partner.html. Accessed 20 Jan. 2019.

Doherty, Thomas. "To Catch a Filmmaker: The Girl, Hitchcock, and Hitchcock." Cineaste, Spring 2013, pp. 4–7.

Dolinh, Alino. "Hitchcock's Portrayals of Women, Intimacy, and Sexual Violence." Film School Rejects. 19 Mar. 2018. filmschoolrejects.com/hitchcocks-portrayals-of-women-intimacy-and-sexual-violence/. Accessed 20 Jan. 2019.

The Girl. Role by Toby Jones and Sienna Miller. BBC/HBO, 2012. Directed by Julian Jarrold, HBO, 2012.

Hedren, Tippi. *Tippi: A Memoir*. William Morrow, 2016.

Hiscock, John. "Tippi Hedren Interview: 'Hitchcock Put Me in a Mental Prison.'" *The Telegraph.* 24 Dec. 2012. www.telegraph.co.uk/culture/film/starsandstories/9753977/Tippi-Hedren-interview-Hitchcock-put-me-in-a-mental-prison.html. Accessed 8 Feb. 2013.

Hitchcock. Role by Sir Anthony Hopkins, Helen Mirren, and Scarlett Johansson. The Montecito Picture Co., 2012. Directed by Sacha Gervasi, Fox Searchlight Pictures, 2012.

Lang, Brent. Tippi Hedren Recounts What Happened When She Turned Down Alfred Hitchcock's Advances" *Variety.* 13 Dec. 2017. variety.com/2017/film/news/tippi-hedren-alfred-hitchcock-the-birds-sexual-harassment-1202637959/. Accessed 20 Jan. 2019.

Lowman, Rob. "The other A. Hitchcock was director's wife, Alma." *The Los Angeles Daily News.* 13 Dec. 2012. www.kentucky.com/entertainment/movies-news-reviews/article44393079.html. Accessed 28 Feb. 2013.

Malm, Sara. "Hitchcock star Tippi Hedren says director was 'evil', and she'd be rich if sexual harassment laws applied in the 1960s." www.dailymail.co.uk/news/article-2182804/Hitchcock-star-Tippi-Hedren-says-director-evil-shed-rich-sexual-harassment-laws-applied-1960s.html. 2 Aug. 2012. Accessed 6 Mar. 2013.

Miller, Mark Crispin. "In Memoriam—Alfred Hitchcock (1899–1980)." *The New Republic.* www.newrepublic.com/article/114279/alfred-hitchcocks-hidden-genius.com. 24 Jan. 2019.

O'Connell, Pat Hitchcock and Laurent Bouzereau. *Alma Hitchcock: The Woman Behind the Man.* New York: Berkley Books, 2003.

Oglethorpe, Tim. "Hitchcock? He was a psycho: As a TV drama reveals his sadistic abuse, *Birds* star Tippi Hedren tells how the director turned into a sexual predator who tried to destroy her." *Daily Mail,* 2012, www.dailymail.co.uk/tvshowbiz/article-2251425/Tippi-Hedren-tells-Alfred-Hitchcock-turned-sexual-predator-tried-destroy-her.html. Accessed 21 July 2016.

Rampton, James. "Obsession: The Dark Side of Alfred Hitchcock." Independent. 26 Dec. 2012. www.independent.co.uk/arts-entertainment/films/features/obsession-the-dark-side-of-alfred-hitchcock-8431033.html. Accessed 20 Jan. 2019.

Rebello, Stephen. *Alfred Hitchcock and The Making of Psycho.* Dembner Books, 1990.

Spoto, Donald. *The Dark Side of Genius: The Life of Alfred Hitchcock.* Boston: Little, Brown and Co., 1983.

---. *Spellbound by Beauty: Alfred Hitchcock and his Leading Ladies.* New York: Harmony Books, 2008.

"Tippi Hedren interviewed by the Chiligods Part 1." 13 Mar. 2013. Youtube.com. Accessed 20 Jan. 2019.

Chapter 6

Social Justice and Cultural Landscape in Toni Morrison's *Beloved*

Dr. Maryann P. DiEdwardo

Lehigh University;
University of Maryland Global Campus

To illustrate social justice pedagogy and stylistic writing, this researcher teaches cultural landscape, or place, that mirrors the functionality of the language of metaphor of imaginary places. My students write about their own cultural experiences in places as a preliminary space practice. Further, students approach the study of literary works of those writers who reached them through the language of place or setting. Toni Morrison offers us the vision of a narrative space and the trauma of interior personal space, to share the pain of the ghost of a baby in *Beloved*. The text reveals the literary imagination through the context of the speeches by the dead baby; we envision a narrative space. Death becomes the condition or quality that is transferred with aesthetic action and nature. From useful theoretical models such as semiotics and poetic theory, I interpret the words of Morrison as the signifier of the message of hopelessness. Spatializing the narrative language of Morrison reveals the purpose of crafting a cultural landscape in a particular text which is a hermeneutic approach.

Social justice pedagogy includes powerful pieces, such as *The Bluest Eye* and *Beloved*, by Toni Morrison, a modernist. The literary fiction is cathartic to bring out those students who experience abusive situations. On their own, they quietly reveal their experiences in private ways. Gender status acts as a profound theme in the work of Morrison. Next, the reality of the lack of power of women in history is forever thrust upon the students as they read archival evidence in letters, newspapers, and narratives.

Cultural poetics, intersectionality, intertextuality, modernism, and semiotics function to decipher clues about multiple strands of complexity in *The Bluest Eye* and *Beloved*. Applicable to the study of Morrison, the writing of oneself, the lonely island of the self, represents our search for words to describe situations. Morrison applies poetics as a methodology to capture and apply feminine myth as an island of selfhood in creation of works of fiction, to create the poetics of language, essential to the significance of the messages.

The significance of the message of Morrison's *Beloved* is a signifier of the importance of the spiritual in writing and language. In fact, Morrison creates the voice of a dead child to represent spirituality through myth. Ultimately, writing is a personal journey determined by Baby Sugg's room, which becomes an island place of worship.

"Journaling the Streets" has been a title for my current writing style. I journal about my thinking. Small notebooks and large computer files are part of the project. I try to recall places in books to journal, to teach and to engage in semiotics, or the study of language and literature as signs and indices. I am journaling about the places in the works of Toni Morrison.

Chapter 7

Metacognitive Pedagogy Breaks Down Interpersonal Borders

Dr. Maryann P. DiEdwardo

Lehigh University;
University of Maryland Global Campus

Cultural knowledge of the world is perhaps a useful tool to interpret and to evaluate. Hermeneutics reveals truth, originates with Hermes, the Greek god, and is mostly attributed to the Socratic Method by Plato, which is a claim by Gadamer. In the 20th century, his teacher, Heddeiger, re-envisioned hermeneutics to encompass all fields.

This researcher is experienced in designing learning paradigms and structures online based on the Socratic Method for traditional hybrid and computer-based classes. Writing fiction, nonfiction, poetry, and drama as a learning community, with the Socratic Method, in writing curriculums in distance settings with self-assessments through metacognitive pedagogy can improve student learning and achievement.

The most important outcome of this chapter is efficacy. To prepare, this researcher applies metacognitive processes which aid figuring out how to do a particular set of tasks and ensuring that the processes are performed correctly (Sternberg). Hermeneutic Arc (Framework) copyright Maryann DiEdwardo, Ed.D.: Metacognitive planning; journal; continue chats; deconstruction (Derrida): character impersonation persona monologues: analysis of literary elements; research biographical and historical background; interpret language using Reader-Response Theory, Identity Theory, and New Historicism; connect cultural observations with inclusion of personal narrative; writing process: drafting; submissions; presentations; critique. All communication, such as literature is hermeneutic. Gadamer recaptures hermeneutics. Historicity is vital, since we can inhabit the consciousness of the author. Distinguish scientific knowledge as subjective and other fields may recognize the author's time and space. Texts are meant to be interpreted. Gadamer is interested in the reasoning of the interpreter.

Dietrich Bonhoeffer's hermeneutics defines three parts to Revelation, as faith, love, and Christ, and others such as Dorothy Day, seeks to solve hunger, with even others such as Martin Luther King Jr., Dalai Lama, Mahatma Gandhi, Golda Meir, and Maya Angelou also define hermeneutics by action. Upon his death, Mohandas K. Gandhi was hailed by the London Times. Gandhi protested against racism in South Africa and colonial rule in India by using nonviolent resistance. A testament to the revolutionary power of nonviolence, Gandhi's approach directly influenced Martin Luther King Jr. Philosophical hermeneutics pursues two broad questions that are fundamental to any efforts to transform a society. The first focuses on the culture of individuals within a society, i.e., how does a person interpret the world around them and how does this, in turn, affect the manner in which they come to think and act? Dilthey had sought to resolve this question by putting forward a philosophy of "worldviews," but it was radicalized by Martin Heidegger into the question about the roles understanding and interpretation play in our everyday lives: they are in fact constitutive of our very being as part of an existential structure known since antiquity and called the "hermeneutic circle," whereby we experience, i.e., understand and interpret anything new on the basis of what we know or believe already. This circle need not be taken as a "vicious" one, so long as writers are aware of it. The second question emerges from the first, in that it asks how two individuals from dissimilar cultures, thinking and acting as differently as they do, can reach common understanding through communication.

This chapter is based on a research project to use metacognition and writing to enhance writing achievement. At the Northeast Modern Language Association Conference in 2017, this researcher presented an original paper titled "Metacognition and Student-Directed Pedagogy in Hybrid and Online Writing Courses" for a Panel: Emerging Pedagogy and Tools for Online Composition and Writing Intensive Courses. The central argument stresses metacognitive activities in all writing settings, from K–adult. Connections between ideas are essential for metacognitive thinking. Working memory is the part of our minds that hold information temporarily for processing. Yet, working memory is quite limited in capacity; we can hold only so much information in our conscious awareness at one time. However, reading skills are fluent, and then the burden of working memory is reduced.

Applying metacognitive pedagogy breaks down interior interpersonal borders. These borders may be internal conflicts that students are experiencing. Globalization of the literary canon requires applications of the aspects of oral history traditions. My class is organized to become a learning community with a focus on writing short stories as authentic assessments to develop student voices. Allow students to write about their lives. Create alternative projects such as writing short stories instead of an essay.

Metacognition refers to higher-order thinking, which involves active control over the cognitive processes engaged in learning. Metacognition is the ability to control one's cognitive processes. Self-regulation has been linked to intelligence. Sternberg refers to these executive processes as metacomponents in his triarchic theory of intelligence. Metacomponents are executive processes that control other cognitive components as well as receiving feedback from these components. Knowing when, where, and how to remember, involves planning, evaluating, and monitoring. Further, metacognitive processes require embedding, informing, and training.

This researcher called upon the students to develop creative blog posts and short presentations about their life stories. Ask questions about hobbies and interests. Background knowledge probes are built on previous or favorite writing. Offer students time to write and add one-minute papers. Create students' voices in class with free writing prompts as metastudy to prepare to write. Create social network journals. Digital revolution projects abound with creative ways to use e-portfolios, WordPress, blogs, e-books, and other methodologies to write and self-publish. The following sample life story has an annotated bibliography, which can also be a collaborative project.

The relationship between modeling methodology and writer identity is essential. There is a connection between literary and cognitive function. The findings from the Nun Study (1930) indicate that the ability to write texts that are "idea dense" may be manifested in the brain in some way and raise intriguing questions about the connection between literacy and cognitive function. They also complicate issues concerning relationship between genre and identity. The genres that the nuns wrote in 1930 were short narratives or stories that addressed biographical content and, presumably, the nuns were familiar with the genres they were expected to produce. But some wrote stories with greater detail (idea density) than others, a finding that raises a number of interesting questions. Another question concerns whether the connection between the ability to write idea-dense texts and Alzheimer's disease was causal or correlational. Did the ability to write idea-dense texts prevent dementia in some way? Or was the poor linguistic ability and dementia related to some other factor that affected both? Although we do not have answers to the complicated issues raised by the Nun Study, current research in neuroplasticity strongly suggests that what we learn and what we do correlate with neuronal activity" (Neuroplasticity, Genre, and Identity 177).

This emphasis on historicity and on the significance of language as a vehicle for interpretive endeavors are key dimensions of Gadamer, who views an awareness of historically informed prejudices as a basic condition of understanding (Kinsella).

Notes

The Fourth "R": A Book to Promote the Journey through Hispanic American Literary History to Develop Language Skills. Bloomington, Indiana: AuthorHouse, 2008. Review: "Dr. DiEdwardo's book is a 'must have' for all educators, especially for those who teach students of other languages. The book is simple, and its components are easy to follow. What I find particularly compelling about this book is the idea to use authors from the students' home country to enhance self-esteem and pride, in addition to creating individual voices."—Toni Velleca, ESOL teacher.

Works Cited

Bruffee, K. A. (1995). Sharing our toys: Cooperative learning versus collaborative learning. *Change,* 27(1), pp. 12–18.

DiEdwardo, Maryann. (2010). *The Fourth R.* Google Books. Online. Available. books.google.com/books/about/The_Fourth_R.html?id=DE5dkaqDpXgC. Accessed 12 Mar. 2012.

---. "Implementing Learning Strategies Based on Metacognition." *Journal of Modern Education Review,* vol. 7, no. 6, June 2017, pp. 380–388. New York: Academic Start, 2017.

---. Living Literacy. Kindle. www.amazon.com/gp/aw/d/1438962215/ref=mp_s_a_1_2?qid=1398650851 &sr=1-2&pi=SY200_QL40.

---. *Metacognition.* Prezi. prezi.com/user/jaylp90n6wuq/.

Flavell, J. H. "Metacognition and cognitive monitoring: A new area of cognitive-developmental inquiry." *American Psychologist,* 34(10), pp. 906–911, 1987.

---. "Speculation about the nature and development of metacognition." Chapter in F. E. Weinert and R. H. Kluwe (Eds.) *Metacognition, Motivation, and Understanding.* Pp. 21–22,1987.

Frey, Daniel. "Preface." *Paul Ricoeur. Hermeneutics, Writings and Lectures, vol. 2.* Trans. David Pellauer. Massachusetts: Malden, 2016.

Gadamer, Hans-Georg. Weinsheimer, Joel. Trans. *Hermeneutics, Religion, and Ethics.* New Haven: Yale University Press, 1999.

Kaplan, David M. "Discourse and critique in the hermeneutic phenomenology of Paul Ricoeur" (1998). ETD Collection for Fordham University. AAI9816348. fordham.bepress.com/dissertations/AAI9816348.

Kinsella, Elizabeth Anne. *Hermeneutics and Critical Hermeneutics: Exploring Possibilities Within the Art of Interpretation.* iBooks, vol. 7, no. 3, art. 19, May 2006.

Lawless, G. J., Constantineau P., Dizboni A. (2017) Philosophical Hermeneutics and Hermeneutic Philosophy. In: A Hermeneutic Analysis of Military Operations in Afghanistan. Palgrave Macmillan, New York, 24 June 2017, DOI doi.org/10.1057/978-1-137-60012-7_5.

Sternberg in *Interamerican Journal of Psychology,* 2005, vol. 39, no. 2, pp. 189–202, "The Theory of Successful Intelligence," eric.ed.gov/?id=EJ773903.

Timo, Laato. "Romans As the Completion of Bonhoeffer's Hermeneutics." Jets. 58/4, 2015. www.etsjets.org/files/JETS-PDFs/58/58-4/JETS_58-4_709-29_Laato.pdf.

Trainin and Swanson. "Cognition, Metacognition, and Achievement of College Students with Learning Disabilities." *Learning Disability Quarterly,* 2006. files.eric.ed.gov/fulltext/EJ725678.pdf.

Veerman, Elshout, Busato. Metacognitive Meditation in Learning with Computer-Based Simulations. Computers in Human Behavior. 10 (1). 1994, pp. 93–106.

Chapter 8

Biblical Hermeneutics and the Book of Job

Susan Strangeland

Independent Scholar

This chapter will be an exploration into the Book of Job from the Old Testament of the Christian Bible. The history of Job, his story and his experiences during this time in his life. I will be focusing on two aspects of this book and how these aspects have helped me grow spiritually. I will also be discussing the importance of Biblical hermeneutics in today's world.

The Book of Job is the first poetic book of the Old Testament in the Christian Bible and some believe that this was the first book of the Bible to be written. The approximate date of the Book of Job is unknown but records events that occurred during the time of the patriarchs, Abraham, Isaac, Jacob, which would have been between 2000–1800 BC. The story is located in the land of Uz, which was probably located northeast of Palestine, near desert land between Damascus and the Euphrates River. The author is unknown, possibly Job, but others have suggested Moses, Solomon or Elihu.

Job was a prosperous farmer living in the land of Uz. He has thousands of sheep, camels, and other livestock, a large family and many servants. He was the greatest man among all the people of the East. Job was blameless and upright, he feared God and shunned evil (*The Life Application Bible, The New International Version, Job* 1.1). In those days, there were no priests to instruct God's laws, so Job acted as the priest of his family and offered sacrifices to God to ask for forgiveness for sins he and his family had committed. Job did this out of conviction and love for God, not just because of his role as head of the household. In the first chapter, the sixth verse of Job it states "One day the Angels came to present themselves before the Lord, and Satan also came with them. The Lord said to Satan, "Where have you come from?" Satan answered the Lord, "From roaming through the earth and going back and forth in it." The Lord then asks Satan, "Have you considered my servant Job? There is no one on Earth like him; he is blameless and upright, a man who fears God and shuns evil. "Does Job fear God for nothing?" Satan replied. "Stretch out your hand and strike everything he has, and he will surely curse you to your face." The Lord then said to Satan, "Very well, then, everything he has is in your hands, but the man himself do not lay a finger."

Satan originally was an Angel of God, but he became corrupt through his own pride. He has been evil since his rebellion against God and thrown out of Heaven. As a created being, Satan has definite limitations and does his best to tempt anyone he can away from God. In Genesis chapter 3, verse 1, Satan arrives in the garden of Eden to tempt Eve to eat the fruit of the tree of life. Temptation is Satan's invitation to give in to his kind of life and move away from God and all that God has in store for us. Not only did Satan tempt Eve, but in Luke chapter 4, verse 2, he tempted Jesus in the desert for 40 days and 40 nights.

During Job's first test from Satan, he lost his livestock, his sons and daughters and his servants. Job tore his robe at this news and shaved his head, but did not sin by charging God with the wrongdoings (Job 1.22). On another day, the angels came to present themselves to the Lord and Satan also came with them. The Lord asked Satan "where have you come from?" Satan answered, "From roaming through the earth and going back and forth in it." The Lord again said to Satan, "Have you considered my servant Job? There is no one on earth like him." "Skin for skin" Satan replied. "A man will give all he has for his own life, but stretch out your hand and strike his flesh and bones and he will surely curse you to your face." The Lord replied, "Very well, then he is in your hands, but you must spare his life." This is Satan's second test to Job to see if he will curse God for all he has lost. Satan afflicted Job with painful sores from the soles of his feet to the top of his head. Job still did not sin in what he said about God. Satan had to seek permission from God to inflict pain upon Job. God limits Satan and in this case, God did not allow Satan to destroy Job.

In these first two chapters of Job, we see God and Satan conversing about God's most willing servant Job. God knows Job's heart and is not tempted by Satan's plan to destroy Job's life and health. God knows that Job will never curse God or blame God for his misgivings. Job has lost almost everything. His family, his livestock, and his health. God shows great love and faith in his servant Job, enough faith that when Satan comes and tests Job's faith, God has no doubts that Job will stay true. The message of Job is that you should not give up on God because he allows you to have bad experiences. Faith in God does not guarantee personal health or prosperity.

The next thirty-six chapters of Job are full of discussion between Job and his friends about what has happened and who is to blame. In chapter 38.1, God finally answers Job out of a storm. Job's friends had not spoken kindly about God and what they thought God had done to Job. God rebuke's Job's three friends, Eliphaz, Bildad and Zophar, for adding to Job's suffering by their false assumptions and critical attitudes towards God. They were told to take seven bulls and seven rams and go to Job and sacrifice a burnt offering for yourselves (Job 42.9). God says "My servant Job will pray for you, and I will accept his prayer and not deal with you accordingly to your folly." They did as they were told and the Lord accepted Job's prayer for his friends. After Job had prayed for his friends, the Lord made him prosperous again and gave him twice as much as he had before (Job 42.10) This is a beautiful example of praying for others in God's name. God listens to our call. God was not willing to forgive Job's friends, they needed to be forgiven from Job first, then God was willing to forgive. Job lived a hundred and forty years after he was tested by Satan. The Lord blessed the latter part of Job's life more than the first.

The importance of Biblical hermeneutics in this chapter of Job has been the study of the principles that I have interpreted while reading Job. The relationship between God, and Satan, who seems to appear out of nowhere. God and Satan talk for a moment and God brings up his servant Job. It is Satan that asks God, "Does Job fear God for nothing?" (Job 1.9) The opportunity that God gives Satan to destroy all the Job has without harming Job. Job loses his family, his servants and his livestock, his whole life has been destroyed. Satan then returns to God for a second time and God again asks Satan about Job. Satan is again allowed to put painful sores all over Job from his feet to his head. Out of all this anguish, Job never curses God, he stays his loyal servant. There are such wonderful lessons here and in all the books of the Bible. The Bible is the living word of God. There isn't a time that I don't open the Bible to study and learn something new, something that I may have missed or wasn't ready to see. As we grow and change, the stories become richer and more complex. As I grow spiritually, I sit and wait for the word of God to speak to me, to show me how to live. The Christian Bible has been my study guide for the last twenty-five years and in those years, I have deepened my faith and my relationship with God and his greater purpose for my life.

In this chapter, I have discussed parts of the Book of Job that I find compelling. The relationship between good and evil. Faith and suffering. There is wealth, health and livelihood, then total destruction. The story takes us on a difficult journey of a servant of God and all that he is willing to go through to remain so. It is in God's grace that there is restoration of Job's life, and even more blessings than prior to his testing. Shall we all be so lucky.

Works Cited

The Life Application Bible, The New International Version. Tyndale House Publishers, Incorporated and Zondervan Publishing House, 1988.

Chapter 9

Reflections from a Reading Classroom

Dr. Juliet Emanuel

Borough of Manhattan Community College

Putting a name to it.

The question was unexpected. "But what I want to know," the interrogator said, "was how did she (the student) get from that first essay to the last. What happened?"

This was a question that in its composition questioned the student, the instructor, the levelling of academic plateaus, indeed seemed to get to the gist of knowledge of a strategy in all its derivation and practice. That it occurred just as the question-and-answer period after a set of presentations by composition teachers was ending was actually a relief.

I have been teaching by analyzing student work, not by consciously applying theories or their derivations to the processes and practices that I used. Indeed, such was the measured speed with which I had to work that I barely had enough time to accommodate all the dissonant voices in my classroom and to bring all the students to the place where they felt comfortable facing the dreaded college and university mandated final examinations in either writing or reading.

However, let me set the stage for you.

The community college in which I have taught for many years is part of a large system located in a major metropolitan area in the east of the United States of America. The institution that forms the locus of this paper is noted in its website to house students from more than 155 countries. Any class for which I am the instructor may have representatives from any of those countries. Thus, the students are likely to have one thing in common: limited vocabulary in English.

The question posed to me and noted above was not a rhetorical one. It demanded an answer, or at least some consideration, then. It was related to the theme being discussed in this set of essays. In this paper, I will attempt to analyze years of instruction during which the precepts linked to hermeneutics, metacognition, and writing, in retrospect, were identifiable. There will be four case studies, each of which will illustrate the methods used to address the discrete sections of the prescribed syllabus mandated by the department in which these courses are held. One case study will have as its focus a composition course.

Further, in each case, because of the specifics related to the Developmental Skills Department, now known as Academic Literacy and Linguistics, and the component for which this writer is the instructor, and the English Department, the writing of the composition was not mandatory. Composition was the determination of the English Department.

Text one: I teach reading

The process of reading is intangible, varied, and confounding McGraw and Mason in 2019.

We read in the language of English, recognized as one of the loci of cultural power, the 1992 book by Phillipson titled *Linguistic Imperialism.*

These two references are, even with time between them, a subtext to the course which I have been teaching for three decades. English has become the preferred langue in business, education, sociology, and the many areas in which the students of the metropolitan area hope to be understood and to be successful. The vibrant research done over the past two decades by the International Association dedicated to the study of World Englishes gives an indication of the multilinguistic variations of what in some communities is still termed "the mother tongue." It is, however, within this multiplicity of variations on "mother tongue" that the necessary study of the students is based.

Let us continue then with stating that the practical observations and materials for this paper arise from the needs of students for whom several forms of English are brought to the classroom. In this classroom, the students are to accommodate themselves not only to specific words related to content courses, but also to entire sets of words that are needed for them to negotiate living in various sections of a most diverse city, the diversity of which is seen in the classrooms of the college and in the instructors themselves.

Foundationally, the reading course has not emphasized writing as part of its syllabus. Writing and any composition of text or examination of the composing process was and still is, to some degree, the choice of the instructor. The students, several years ago, had to pass a high-stakes examination, a standardized test. In reading, not in composition.

Case study #1: Suni

Suni had been placed in the highest level of the reading sequence. This meant that she had demonstrated proficiency in reading English at least at a ninth-grade level. This was not her first enrollment in this section of reading. Several of the students had bonded along cultural lines and it was one student in particular who lobbied for Suni. Clearly, Suni worked hard in class. She had been a famous artist in China, according to her classmates, and was distressed that advanced proficiency in English was eluding her.

Early in the semester, I ask students to submit a composition in which they described when and how they first learned to read. Reading their writing helps me to follow not only the path each had followed educationally, but also to put together a set of exercises particular to each of them, and as necessary. Periodically I bring in one or two very short essays from *The Open Door, When Writers First Learned to Read*, by Steven Gilbar. We read about the early struggles of these geniuses, such as Charles Dickens, Jean Rhys, Winston Churchill, and Frederick Douglass, and this is the first of confidence-building experiences among the students. They delighted in reading about Winston Churchill's experience in learning to read and do sums.

> It was at the "Little Lodge" I was first menaced with Education. The approach of a sinister figure described as "the Governess" was announced. The arrival was fixed for a certain day. In order to prepare for this day Mrs. Everest produced a book called *Reading without Tears*. It certainly did not justify its title in my case. I was made aware that before the governess arrived I must be able to read without tears. We toiled each day. … I thought it all very tiresome our preparations were by no means completed when the fateful hour struck and the governess was due to arrive. I did what so many oppressed peoples have done in similar circumstances, I took to the woods (Churchill 3–4).

Indeed, how many children have not run away or tried to on the second day of kindergarten!

After such a reading, then the students of the class are off to write their own essays on their first encounters with reading. Suni did not submit hers. The students told me that she was afraid to do so and wanted to make a good impression.

When I did ask her for the essay, she showed me the notebook filled with a range of vocabulary that she thought she would need to explain herself to me. I asked her to write, then, for me. I assured her that it did not matter how she wrote. I just wanted to see what she wrote.

When Suni presented her essay, it was one of those days when the business of the classroom meant that she could quietly slip me two pages. I thanked her and assured her that I would return the essay by the time the class met again.

What Suni wrote

If hermeneutics may be defined as understanding the meaning, explicit and implicit in word and text, then Suni was already grappling with that element. In her drive for meaning or her "struggle for voice,' she was entering into a stage of metacognition that conclusively drove me to examine my own thought processes.

When she was a child, she wrote, in a period euphemistically termed The Cultural Revolution, Suni and her friends dared to oppose the regime. They understood the risks that they were taking. They knew the consequences. Yet she, and her comrades, dared to hold fast to the passions that motivated their intellect. One of these passions was art: the composition of a narrative that not only recorded what they were experiencing but where they hoped to be one day. With no tools for their trade and its practice, these children, wanting to understand, à la Leonardo, what caused action and connection within each part of the physical body, explored the one place where they could and did find the answers. They ventured into cemeteries and there observed the innards of bodies. The bodies were there, for it was a time of persecution, and retribution to opposition was swift. Perhaps their youth saved them from being discovered and as Suni wrote, she was using that same inquiry and determination in her pursuit of English now. She examined in order to understand; she recorded the smallest details to gather their significance. She learned that she was an artist (the Cultural Revolution had failed by the time she was in her very early teens) by dissecting, assessing, and constructing connections by taking out of a dark place the qualities needed to create by brush a composition.

I asked her if she had any copies of her work. Actually, I used the word "portfolio," for no other reason than as an immigrant myself, I recognized that one kept a body of work either in a hard copy or in memory. For Suni it was both: she brought in a small notebook. It was filled with wondrous things.

Each month during the academic year, the college celebrates, as part of its commitment to diversity, a heritage month. Because my Cantonese was nonexistent and Suni's spoken English was as limited, we needed an interpreter to negotiate our dialogue. We found two, both in positions of power in the college administration and those placements were revelatory to Suni. After a visit to both, Suni was tasked to produce a piece of art representative of Asian Heritage Month. As we left these meetings, Suni remarked with carefully chosen words that she did not know people like those had such leadership roles in the college.

About two weeks later, Suni appeared at the door of the classroom in which I was teaching and unveiled her painting. Students gasped. This was not the class in which she was enrolled. We asked her to explain the narrative. She did. When she could not find the words, we asked her to gesticulate. There was a lot of help from students with whom she was not familiar, as they gave their voice in recognition of the talent of one of their peers. For what Suni had done was paint herself as a child against the darkness of a regime. Red permeated parts of the work and a very young girl was seated, backing the darkness and reading.

The painting is housed "upstairs." As the days went by, I watched Suni understand her own development. It was not that she did not know the process of understanding and grappling with one's cognition, but in a new context receiving approbation for that process proved the catalyst. This multi understanding of transmission of connectivity brought Suni into a new place of being.

I have attempted to record and analyze Suni's experience over the years. I have been advised to examine the work of Cathy Caruth on trauma theory. While some of Caruth's early investigation about woundedness has been discarded, it served as a starting point for much of the openness about the effects of psychic and physical abuse, and the need for a voice and understanding of the struggle for an approbation of self and respect for the struggle for being. Today Suni has been an academic tutor. Validation of her life experience gave her a self-reported confidence and it is that assurance that promoted positivity in the performance of her studies.

Suni's story, truncated here necessarily, is not as unusual as it may seem. In the typical classroom in the college where these experiences take place, it would be strange not to find traumatic experiences. When a student reaches out, then one sits quietly and listens. Perhaps that is all that is needed to get beneath the fear of a multi-city of new "livings." From a country of knowing, where however disturbing the circumstances, one is part of the landscape, to one of unknowing and hope where there does not seem to be a center to one's daily life, disruption needs assistance. Indeed, negotiation of the field before them is composed of new peripheries and an often only dreamed-about center. How then does an instructor find the key to hermeneutics, metacognition, and, ultimately, writing among a class of students new to the culture of the country, state, city, or classroom?

Reading out loud

Aya Matsuda, in a recent presentation at the 24th International Conference of the International Association for World Englishes, in her paper, "Evolving Roles of Literature Courses in EIL, English as an International Language, Teacher Preparation Courses," examines how literature contributed to the planned syllabi of these pedagogues. The concern to the presenter was how much diversity and breadth there was among the texts selected for inclusion in the course materials, either at the teacher preparation level or the student curriculum level. She discussed the need for materials that cut across national boundaries and that are relevant to the global society, fostering thus a sense of global citizenship. Multi-themed literature has been used in classrooms. Nevertheless, with the slow incursion of multilinguistic variations in English, especially in the metropolitan institution forming the locus for this paper, the discussion seems jejune. The syllabi for classes such as the one in which Suni was enrolled have long included "additional readings." However, students already saturated by increasingly incessant media chatter, are compelled many times to forgo study in order to make a living, forced to recognize that indeed one can make it in New York, but not without work that is time-consuming and onerous, and have little patience with "literary works"—translation: a novel of many pages or an anthology of similar heft. With some of them already qualified for major professions in their countries of birth, only a nuanced knowledge and acquisition of English separates them from achieving the American Dream. The dream has this reality: hard work and no leisure time. As immigration patterns change, so do the class materials, in my case. While Flaubert's *Madame Bovary* was a good fit two decades ago for a mostly English-speaking class—albeit it at less than proficiency level—it had become less so for a class of twenty-six speaking possibly an equivalent number of languages. In addition, the passage of time had allowed for a technologically based apparent familiarity with other cultural histories. Nevertheless, with the commonplace homogeneity of lived lives came a blunting of emotion that revealed itself in her essay that was Suni's first written class assignment. Suni's closure of memory contained a dichotomy: as a child in the absence of the schoolroom, she dealt with the dead bodies of persons whom she may have known, in order to concentrate on the ability to draw, in a fairly clinical setting, and in order to live in America, she had blunt recall of that which had prompted her own learning. It should come as a surprise to no one that one part of the practice of her craft lay in the film industry as she created sets. For the artificiality of the set itself reveals a negation and a pretense at living in truth.

The inclusion of instructor-chosen literature in a given syllabus for a semester has been as varied as the lived experiences of the students comprising a class. The students may choose, outside of the required textbook in the strategies of comprehension, among the recommended adjunct readings. While periodically these readings are chosen because of current events, they are predominantly selected with an eye toward accessibility in comprehension and towards continuance in the content areas of the years of study ahead of them. In addition, students may choose their own books. Since the college is located in downtown Manhattan, familiarity of the neighborhood has lent itself to a changing landscape of gentrification, with its concomitant removal of spaces that celebrated the immigrant experience. One text that spoke to the early immigrant experience, with all its brutality, in that locality has been *Maggie: A*

Girl of the Streets. Variously the text lent itself to discussions about life among those who lived in poor neighborhoods and the determination to remove oneself from that milieu; to aspects of parenting; of love and marriage; of family structures; options; responsibilities; and gender-driven explorations. It also helped that Stephen Crane had an interesting life and died young. During those semesters when students did not find his approximation of dialect in *Maggie: A Girl of the Streets* easy to understand, a more accessible text has been another of Stephen Crane's short novels, *The Open Boat.* Situated as it is on the banks of a river with New Jersey within sight on the other shore, it is easy to explore vicariously the balance between Human and Nature and the unpredictability of life. The purpose of any literary selection is to promote both dialogue and conversation, to find commonalities; to explore and reflect on not only the text but what is the process behind the text itself. While not all pieces of literature are suitable for those whose previous experiences lie buried or are just below the surface of their smiles, some students have allowed discussions that show the various mindsets and belief patterns among students. Such a piece would be Jamaica Kincaid's *Girl.* Frequently, *Girl* is used as a feminist text. The discussions are vibrant as students share experiences about their own strict mother figures for whom they felt a mixture of awe and fear. Not unusual, however, is the response to the short prose poem that takes the opposite tack: this is a very good mother teaching her daughter how to be a good woman. Another such selection would be *The Chronicle of a Death Foretold.* For the purpose of this paper, I must mention that the practice of honor killing, which is the nexus of *The Chronicle of a Death Foretold,* has been considered very carefully, as it is a subject close to the reported cultural practice of some students. Such a text must be carefully considered lest it strikes too close to the center of a specific student's own mode of experience. The aim of any such explicatory session is not to ruffle feathers, but to bring along the students to a point where a discussion and an argument are possible, and where denial and clarification of preconceived notions are viable. The text must be easy to understand, plot-wise, and the language of the text must create openings for an understanding of rhetorical devices, characterizations, action, and, very subtly at this point in their college careers, place in the canon.

Let us briefly return to *The Open Boat.*

First, let us note that for these novellas and short stories as chosen above, reading aloud may be done. While I may model a piece of reading text, the students are encouraged to read aloud. The mode has a twofold purpose: to help with concentration on the text as it evolves and to promote comprehension, vocabulary introduction, and advancement and other elements related to the act of reading in English. One remark comes to mind.

As the class listened to their classmate reading the story in *The Open Boat* of the protagonists who were paddling a lifeboat towards shore during a fierce storm, they appeared intent on what they were reading.

The boat had been pushed back once more by the storm and, as tired as they were, the four men in the boat kept going. Then the student who was reading, said quietly, "Determination. When you want something, then sometimes you have to push forward for that prize." To which another said, "Sometimes you do not grasp the prize."

They were teaching themselves. Quietly they either creased the top corners of the page being read or placed marks next to the relevant text on the page.

Indeed, what the second had recognized was that death was imminent, or what, then, would be the purpose of the tale. There would have to be a climax.

Subtext: The summary is formally required.

The practice of summarizing is, according to some writers of textbooks, hard to teach and equally difficult for students to practice initially. Yet, as may be seen in the instance mentioned above, an attempt was made to grasp the gist of a novella and to attempt the act of annotation. This precise incident occurred before the department instituted a summarization exercise as part of the final assessment of the course. Indeed, as has been pointed out in class, we summarize all the time. The statement that one has had a bad day or a good day is a summary of a set of events taken in their order of importance and relevance to one's actions throughout a period of time. One ignores the smaller irritants or successes and records the major ones. It is then the ability to see this facility to summarize in what is termed "foreknowledge" that makes the process of summary easier.

From their reflection and mine, I know they have taken the text and made it theirs; that they are on their way to becoming readers. Here, I may give a list of short pieces; for example, *The Stolen Party* by Liana Heker, or longer selections, such as *Push* by Sapphire. Sometimes, a student recommends a piece of literature to me. Among these have been *The Woman in the Dunes* by Kobo Abe and *Requiem for a Woman's Soul* by Omar Rivabella. I have asked for reviews from any source, their own or a critic's. The ones for *Requiem for a Woman's Soul* were not quite positive.

It helps very much if a writer is available to visit a class.

Case study #2: Here comes a poet.

April sometimes sees the celebration of Poetry Month on the campus. On occasion, I have invited a poet whose work fits in with the centrality of the materials chosen for that semester, to introduce his work to a class. Elvis Alves, using his debut poetry collection, was glad to oblige. It helped that he was very young, attractive, and able to draw the students into his world. He explained his motivation, work ethic, profession, education, and then asked permission of the students to read from his collection. Of interest to the students was his decision to make a statement about the poem before he read it. He explained that his mother had approved of the poem. The students were intrigued.

Bitter Melon, the three-part poem by Elvis Alves, gives his book its title and is an exegesis on his mother's life. Here it is, excerpted for brevity.

Bitter Melon (Two)

Diced pieces of a canoe shaped vegetable cook to perfection, green becomes brown when tomato sauce mixes with minced garlic, chopped onion, salt, black pepper, assorted spices,

dressed with oil in a bubbling pot.

Bitter melon is an acquired taste; something to grow into like an oversized pair of shoes.

"You will learn to love her," my mother says, as she throws pinches of curry powder into the simmering pot with the left hand and stirs its contents with a wooden spoon held in the right hand.

The rapid genuflections of her hand remind me of the action of a Hindu woman dipping and throwing specks of gold dust held in a bowl atop the bared heads of jhandi flags as these symbols of faith and

good fortune dance in the wind, dodging the flakes thrown at them.

Bitter melon is gold of the food world that nobody desires, I think but do not say aloud, wondering if my mother had learned to love my father by the time I was born.

In 2015, Chris Cummings writes, in "Engaging New College Students in Metacognition for Critical Thinking: A Developmental Education Perspective," that many educators at the college level recognize this and expect students to demonstrate critical thinking early in their college experience. … Further, research calls for the incorporation of teaching metacognition as a tool for engaging in critical thinking in 2007 by McKinney and 2014 by Pelton; instructors who do not address this call may be leaving new students in a struggle to adapt to the demands of college.

When Elvis Alves had finished reading the poem, the students gave him a standing ovation. Earlier in the session, they had asked him the necessary questions for a comprehension of Alves as a poet and a young person. Their minds had been made receptive to his life experiences and what J. Brooks Bouson calls collective secrets. And perhaps we are closer here to what Stuart Hall terms speaking through the experience itself. Trauma is not just an unrepresentable event, one not solvable, but it is a life event, triggers notwithstanding, that students appreciate as part of a trajectory that places each of them in a necessary reading or writing developmental course. Is this, then, a necessary epistemology? Has permission to voice the event, according to one's own linguistic apparatus, such as Alves does through a conversation with his mother, a dialogue laden with references to an arranged and possibly loveless marriage that brings forth a son, "Woman, here is your son" in the caption and the term, the flakes of gold, plus the words that resonate after that quote from John (*Authorized King James Version* John 19.26) "In whom I am well pleased" enough to heal or at least cover the wound? His words had become theirs by osmosis. They would soon find their own. They think, but they do say aloud. Will they write?

The students received the experience, joining the poet through his words, in a context that was not only familiar to them, but it set up a model which they may imitate. For many of the students, if not all, in a class to which the word "multicultural" may easily be applied, the preference for a boy child would not be an unusual event.

Neither had been given a lesson on metacognition, using that precise term, yet each grasped the layered process that went into an examination of the production of comprehension within that most highly intuitive, nuanced of languages, English. Through Suni's painting, they recognized the darkness of a cultural revolution that ultimately was recognized as a failure. From this darkness, she had emerged successful. Through Alves, they understood that he was the light that a resilient mother had produced and that he was seeking advice from a woman who did not love her husband at the beginning of her marriage. In addition, his use of the words, genuflect, a term used in a Christian to show reverence, and jhandi flags, a Hindu term representing thanksgiving for success and in homage to the Lord Rama and the rescue of his wife Sita by Hanuman from captivity from Rawan, attested to his biculturalism. The examination, then, of these two works of art and the critical, physical responses demonstrated an understanding of the events, wounded though they seemed to be. In both presenters there was pride and confidence in their subsequent achievements.

Would the students be able to replicate the step-by-step processing that they had literally enjoyed or would they be able to respond in writing about what they had encountered?

Would they be able to dissect an event and, having done so, compose a response to that event? Would they be able to go from first to last?

John Flavell generally considered the primary pundit in the general field of cognition in education, stated that metacognition is the knowledge one has about one's own cognitive processes. In addition, he posited that one's ability to reflect upon the tasks and processes one undertakes and to select and utilize the appropriate strategies are both necessary in one's intercultural interactions. Feelings and emotions define one's stages of thinking, and alteration in a state, an opinion, a fact, or any evidence may change a stance that one previously held.

As mentioned before, the student population of the community college defines diversity. Therefore, students who may be defined as those with learning disabilities may be part of a student set within a given classroom. Recently it is to the Learning Disabilities Association of Ontario and its website that I have turned for support in teaching this group.

Contemporary technology therefore serves as the place of resource and research for someone in my field. The now prominent Centers for Excellence in Teaching Learning and Scholarship (CETLS), at this tertiary level, supplement any courses in education to provide an entrance to the very necessary practice of teaching even at the "ivory towered" level. The variety of cultures—ethnic, racial, social, psychological, emotional, physical, and others—calls for an awareness of interaction among these sectors and the often intangible, subtle relationships in the classroom, an awareness the sensitivity of which may periodically be at bay. CETLS and its programs help.

Because of the subtlety of the vernacular of English, it is sometimes difficult for students to grasp the word without a more concrete representation such as Suni's painting of the referents in the example from Alves's poetry. Therefore, when a short story such as "Miss Brill" by Katherine Mansfield, with its painful rendition of ageism, or Jean Rhys's "I Used to Live Here Once," with its portrayal of crossing the metaphoric River Styx, is placed before them, they may read it literally until encouraged to see exactly what the writer is trying to explore. Again, this initial lack of in-depth understanding may go back to grasping the connotations of words as opposed to the exact definitions of the vocabulary. Among the more difficult exercises for students without advanced experience in inferential language, use are those using figurative language and those dealing with tone. For each culture contains its own ways of being. What is humorous in one may not be in another. Students are crossing in subtle ways from one culture into another as they become increasingly facile with English and the varying degrees of feeling and response. The surprise at the scorn of the young couple for the elderly Miss Brill often has led to discussions about respect and honor for the elderly in some non-Western societies. And the protagonist who does not seem to want to leave her earthly boundaries has caused some to question reincarnation and other after-death beliefs.

In an unacknowledged manner at the time, then, metacognition made itself felt. The term, as I mentioned, did not arise, for I had not learned it yet.

Nevertheless, the present reflection gives rise to the following:
Case study #3

In a not unusual move, one of our colleagues had penned a textbook that reached a basic of the expressed needs of our students.

In his introduction to the instructor, the author stated: "The main feature of *Ideal Vocabulary for Reading and Writing: A Novel Approach*, is a story, 'Trial of Love,' that is used as one approach to teach vocabulary."

Further, in his introduction to the students, he advises:

> Our understanding of language controls our ability to interact with the people around us. By improving our skills as listeners, readers, speakers, and writers, we open ourselves to deeper, more meaningful discussions and relationships. We become more effective communicators and listen attentively to what others have to say when our vocabulary is broad and rich. Strong words take us on a journey to "greater." In short, vocabulary really matters.

Clearly, the author, through this text, had the intention of encouraging the students to take in as much vocabulary as possible. More than 1,500 words had been culled from recommended lists, from various sources, including Averil Coxhead's *A New Academic Word List*, and vocabulary websites such as dictionary.com LLC 2014, among others, were used.

The chapter titles were tantalizing: for example, "What Was Mark Doing at Kamla's Home When Her Parents Were at Work?" and "Coming to America."

Included throughout the text are vocabulary exercises offering the students opportunities to figure out unfamiliar words, and they are followed by short reader response exercises.

The characters possessed names that were, in some cases, quite sly, among them Senator Rex, Ronald Spinster, Andrew Stevenson, Dibagio Alexander, and Harley Davidson. In the first chapter, the students were introduced to Sonny,

Rita, and Kamla Kumar, new to America, and Fernandez and Jaime, experienced in border details connected to America.

The use of the word "novel" in the title gave rise to an initial exploration of the denotations and connotations that are basic to the structure of English. It is this multi levelling of definition that bedevils some encountering the language, even at an advanced level. By chapter 4 of the text, the students had stopped reading the story part, as attractive as the story was thought to be, and were concentrating laboriously on the vocabulary exercises themselves. The Pre-Reading and Reader Response sections, if they were attempted at all, were haphazardly done. The struggle became one in which students thought they had to isolate vocabulary and force-feed it to themselves. This was similar to what Suni had been doing. There was, then, no attempt to use the story as a vehicle toward word retention or understanding. The reading out of class was too much and an attempt to read aloud in class was onerous. One part of the reader response exercises should have allowed them to attempt to examine character using action, qualities, and commentaries to make these judgments. The figures were flat to the students. Therefore, we turned the text into a play.

We staged the reading. Characters were chosen by volunteers, and then the readings started. Because in the text each of the characters was given a brief description—for example, Maria, a nurse in the nursing home, and Errol, a taxi driver—each actor offered a description as to what or how the character should be delineated, based on what was known about such characters in real life. Also, in the broadest of descriptions provided by the author, Kamla Kumar is described by the author of the text as a young Indian research scientist and college professor. Although she has a good life in India, she decides to move to America illegally, hoping to advance her career and win a Nobel Prize. Her parents place great value on family and cross the border with her.

The class response was almost magical, for the dramatizations lay not with the story, but with its interpretation and reception of the vocabulary used by the novelist. This was familiar terrain—immigration, the aspirations towards the American Dream, nurses in nursing homes, taxi drivers, and so on. Thus, students read their parts, then, with fresh insight into the characters and the plot and action of the narrative. Of vital importance was the role of the audience. For them, meaning was derived in two ways: one as listeners and readers and another as critics. It was that latter position that accelerated comprehension and placed each student on task. Understudies were only too glad to jump in if an actor was missing—something that rarely happened. Students were intent on task and self-corrected or very gently corrected what they surmised was a misinterpretation of language; in other words, as they read, they applied critical thinking skills. The story built in its action and so did the evolution of the comprehension of the events before them. Based on what they had read, they were able to predict, to analyze, to criticize. They discussed fact and opinion as expressed by what was essentially a piece of prose fiction. The exercises, according to their self-reporting, became easier to work on as foreknowledge, in many cases, had been applied to the text. It did help that the story resonated with many of them, with its tale of immigration struggles, love, betrayal, and the search for the American Dream. Primarily, the reading of the novel section of the text was done in class and this was a task the students decided to have remained there.

Maria Aristodemou comments in her seminal treatise, *Law and Literature: Journeys from Her to Eternity*, that: "Although literature cannot pretend to remedy injustices to the other on the everyday material level, its capacity to help us appreciate, understand, and empathize with what is not ourselves is a starting point to other forms of legislation" (Aristodemou).

Here, let us "legislate," through a textbook created by a well-meaning member of the academy, an entrée to those elusive undertones in English.

Where, say, in the case of a play such as *Romeo and Juliet* where the action, plot, and characterizations are the primary examinations required of the text, in *Ideal Vocabulary, for Reading and Writing: A Novel Approach*, the focus was the understanding of vocabulary by using context, word parts, etc. By facilitating narrative and making it more accessible to the students, with as many of them as possible contributing to the reading of the text, the words gave meaning to themselves, to a sense of passage. And in a more general manner, this form of exercise promoted a community in the class. For ease with comprehension became a class exercise. Confidence was contagious. The instructor's voice diminished. Discussion of each chapter was vital and vigorous. Fact? Opinion? This, as noted before, was somewhat part of their daily lives and so it was not unusual to have students bringing in newspaper clippings or references to films or other tales in support of what they were reading. Easily, then, they were providing supporting evidence for any elucidation for the narrative in which they were essentially engaged.

Therefore, the compromise between those vocabulary exercises and reading for understanding and response was a necessary step in order to support student engagement with the word and its implication. For the instructor, who also served as part of the audience in the staged readings, the sense of the text was reciprocal and increased insight into the action of the novel-text was part of this instructor's experience from time to time. Indeed, as Pinnell and Fountas, in their examination of reading, note, responsive teaching is at the core of guided and/or close reading.

Teacher—teach thyself, and then teach others by your example: some simple truths about teaching and learning.

Case study #4

The answer to the question at the beginning of this essay lies in the case study that follows.

Peter Elbow's dictum in *Writing Without Teachers*, that all of us are writers, perhaps underlies the process that I used in a composition class in the English Department. Students were shy about producing any writing at all. They each expressed fears about the university-mandated final writing test and asked repeatedly for sample examinations and practice in responding to these prompts. They were at the end before we had considered the beginning. There was no prescribed textbook and so I was free to examine responses to ones similar to those I would use in a reading class: When did you first start to write? Do you write now?

As a class, we explored writing in various rhetorical styles over the course of several weeks. Generally, the pieces were produced after readings which became increasingly longer as the weeks progressed. We had gotten to the point where we would read our essays aloud and offer opinions on the content. Criticism was gentle, as we were all writing what we knew, not what was expected by others.

The next exercise was to assess our composition elements for ourselves. I shared that perhaps because of my own early training, I wrote long sentences into which tropical imagery might be inserted. For this reason, I added, I found Faulkner easy to read, with his long stream-of-consciousness sentences. I also shared that one of my professors saw scriptural allusions from various religions in my own writing. Again, coming from a country where three religions were actively practiced and enjoyed by everyone, this sort of use of figurative language and sentence construction was, to me, natural. I wrote what I knew, especially when under pressure. I asked the students to choose any six to four of their favorite pieces of writing and search for images commonly occurring within them.

If I may refer to Alves and his comment about finding and recognizing his voice as a writer, I was asking them to claim their own methods of expressing themselves. I asked them to share, if they wished, what they had written.

Student #1: "I have missed my mother. I did not realize that I wrote so much about her and family."

"Why," asked another student, "did you miss her so much? Is it because you are here and she is there?"

"In a sense, yes. My mother died when I was young, but no one told me how she died."

There was a silence.

Student #1 was perhaps the most sparkling of my students. Effervescent, she lit up the room when she came in. She admitted that she struggled when she came to put pen to paper. Somehow, she could not say what she truly wanted to. Her essays were usually short.

Student #2: "I write a lot about silver. I like moonlight. The best book I ever read was *The Moonlight Bride*."

Student from audience: "Why do you like the book?"

Student #2: "In *The Moonlight Bride* an albino is welcomed as a precious person into a family."

Another student: "But why?"

"Because in her country she was so different, she was a threat. Well, that is what I got from the book. I see also that I constantly use shades of white and write about waves and so on. Different, but good."

Another student: "Did you read Whitman?"

"Who is Whitman?"

"Out of the sea endlessly rocking."

"Oh."

Another student: "Who wrote the book about the bride?"

"Buchi Emecheta."

Student #3: "I saw where it did not matter what the assignment was. I found a way to refer to the landscape, to the earth and the sky and even to birds, such as parrots. I guess I am homesick, but I don't really think so. I just write what I know."

Student from the class: "We are going to take you to the Bronx Zoo. Lots of birds and palms there."

Lots of laughter from the class.

Each student reported on his or her writing.

Assessing their own work and allowing their eyes to "see" what their pens had captured had unlocked a sense of their ability to control both the composing process and their own writing about their lives and the value in those lives. The approbation came from the approval of their peers and from themselves. Here in a community made up of students for whom not one was a speaker of English as a first language, there emerged an understanding of universality of emotion and a continuum of experience, be it in South America or Africa. The word may be different, but the experience was similar, even if denoted by different rules.

The class continued with the exercises, increasing in assignment and complexity, with each student having claimed an authentic voice, and ultimately passing the final exam mandated for the course. They had indeed worked very hard and deserved their success. The query at the beginning of this essay resulted from a presentation of the portfolio of writings collected by the students. The intention was not to elevate the instructor, but to demonstrate how hard each student had worked at arranging his or her thoughts cogently into a coherent whole that was pleasing to himself or herself.

As the writing process revealed itself, I was struck by two details: the community that developed and the ease with which the students validated the efforts of their peers. It appeared that even as each of them wrote, each could hear his or her voice in his or her head. They wrote fluently and convincingly.

Text Two

I do not know whether Student #2 in question ever read Walt Whitman or Student #3 ever visited the Bronx Zoo. In my own experience analyzing my reading and writing practice, I discovered over the years that shift happens. And this as it should be. History, exposure to new experiences, and social imperatives do not permit stasis.

The craft of Jean Rhys, the writer who was born in Dominica and spent most of her adult life in England, is considered one of the most concise practitioners in the crafting of the novel. Her oeuvre, while not large, is remarkable for one long novel, *Wide Sargasso Sea*. This work is considered her response to Charlotte Bronte's *Jane Eyre*, with the latter's rawly unpleasant portrayal of the uprooted West Indian young woman. The generosity of her characterization of Antoinette Cosway, as the first wife of Mr. Rochester, is exemplary. Such is the apparent empathy for the anguish for the young woman that one would expect a corresponding generosity of spirit in all emotions displayed by Rhys. Further, in her finely portrayed description of Selina, another young West Indian and the protagonist in her insightful short story, "Let Them Call It Jazz," one may see a corresponding sympathetic leaning to someone whose life was not evolving exactly as she would have hoped. Nevertheless, her editor, the late Diana Athill, reveals in *Stet*, that a chance remark from Rhys about black people was so startlingly racist that she was puzzled and did wonder if the close relations that the two had developed would have taken place if she had been aware or made aware of Rhys's sentiments. Critical thinking about Rhys's work must accommodate this element in one who is considered among the finest of 20th-century writers.

Is it too much to change the perception of a writer and her or his writing because of a vicious comment?

In commenting on the practice of her craft, in answer to the question: "To what extent, in your view, is writing a political act?" Sarah Ladipo Manyika replied, "To one degree or another, all writing is a political act. I like the way James Baldwin puts it: 'The world changes according to the way people see it, and if you alter, even but a millimeter the way people look at reality, then you can change it.'"

Works Cited

Alves, Elvis. "Bitter Melon," Part Two, *Bitter Melon*. Mahaicony Books, 2013, p. 8.

Aristodemou, Maria. *Law and Literature: Journeys from Her to Eternity*. Oxford UP, 2000.

Athill, Diana, *Stet*. Grove Press, 2002.

Bouson, J. Brooks. *Quiet as It Kept: Shame, Trauma, and Race in the Novels of Toni Morrison*. SUNY Series in Psychoanalysis and Culture, SUNY Press, 1999.

Bronte, Charlotte. *Jane Eyre*. Dover Publications, 2003.

Caruth, Cathy. *Explorations in Memory*. Johns Hopkins UP, 1995.

Churchill, Winston A. *My Early Life: A Roving Commission*. Charles Scribner's Sons, 1930, pp. 3–4.

Crane, Stephen. *Maggie: A Girl of the Streets*. Digireads.com Book, Digireads Publications, 2005.

---. *The Open Boat and Other Stories*. Dover Publications, 1993.

Cummings, Chris. "Engaging New College Students in Metacognition for Critical Thinking: A Developmental Education Perspective." *Research and Teaching in Developmental Education*, vol. 32, no. 1, p. 68–71. 2015, *JSTOR*, www.jstor.org/stable/44290289. Accessed 10 Oct. 2019.

Crystal, David. *Language Death*. Cambridge UP, 2000.

Elbow, Peter. *Writing Without Teachers*. Oxford UP, 1973, 1998.

Emecheta, Buchi. *The Moonlight Bride*. George Braziller, Inc., 1983.

Flaubert, Gustave. *Madame Bovary*. Translated by Margaret Mauldon, Oxford UP 2004.

Flavell, John. "Metacognition and Cognitive Monitoring: A New Area of Cognitive-Developmental Inquiry." *American Psychologist*, 34, pp. 906–911. 10.1037/0003-066X.34.10.906, 1979.

Fountas, Irene and Gay Su Pinnell. *Guided Reading: Responsive Teaching Across the Grades*, 2nd ed. Heinemann, 2016.

Gilbar, Steven. *The Open Door: When Writers First Learned to Read*. David R. Godine Publisher, Inc., 1989.

Hall, Stuart. "Cultural Identity and Diaspora.*" Identity, Community, Culture, Difference*, Edited by Jonathan Rutherford, *Lawrence and Wishart*, 1998, pp. 222–237.

Kincaid, Jamaica. "Girl." *At the Bottom of the River*, Farrar, Straus and Giroux, 1983.

Mansfield, Katherine. *Miss Brill*. www.katherinemansfieldsociety.org Accessed, 3 Oct. 2019.

Manyika, Sarah Ladipo. Twenty Questions with Sarah Ladipo, https://www.the-tls.co.uk/articles/public/twenty-questions-sarah-ladipo-manyika/. Accessed 10 Oct. 2019.

Marquez. Gabriel Garcia. *Chronicle of a Death Foretold*. Alfred A Knopf of Random House Inc., 1983.

Matsuda, Aya. "Evolving Roles of Literature Courses in EIL Teacher Preparation Programs." 24th International Conference, International Association for World Englishes, Limerick, 2019.

Phillipson, Robert. *Linguistic Imperialism*. Oxford UP, 1992.

Rhys, Jean. "I Used to Live Here Once." *The Collected Short Stories*. Norton Paperback Fiction, 1992.

--- *Let Them Call It Jazz and Other Stories*. Penguin, 1995.

--- *Wide Sargasso Sea*. Andre Deutsch, London, 1966.

The Bible. Authorized King James Version. Oxford UP, 1998.

Chapter 10

Francis of Assisi,
A Tale of a Dog and Hermeneutics

Patricia Pasda, B.F.A., M.F.A.

Syracuse University

My service dog, Bolt, served as a balance and seizure dog, all 125 pounds of his beautiful King Shepherd self. Bolt devoted his time to me, watching my every move, and protected the outer sanctuary, his yard and living space. Throughout his life, Bolt never exhibited puppy behaviors, such as chewing shoes or other things that were not his. He ensured that his charge was safe, that the cat who lived with him was happy, and that the small companion dog he had was entertained. Bolt's success with compassion and strength during his lifetime started at his birth and continued in how we lived each day, in the same way our most revered Francis of Assisi calmed and treated the wolf of Gubbio in his lifetime (1180–1226).

Let us first recount the "Legend of the Wolf of Gubbio," in which a healthy wolf ran wild in the region of Umbria, Italy, in the town of Gubbio. The hierarchy of the church asked Francis of Assisi to help the people of Gubbio by attempting to calm the wolf. Francis had already established an order, or group, of peaceful friars in the region, and he was known for kindness to people and animals. In his life before taking the vows of chastity, poverty, and humility, and starting his religious order, he had been a rich young man, a minstrel in his town of Assisi. Francis went to Gubbio and saw not a sick or angry wolf, but a hungry, lonely wolf seeking a way to communicate. The wolf's growls and scratches and attempts at reaching the townspeople were greatly misunderstood. Francis watched and sat by the wolf. He sang and prayed with the wolf. The wolf of Gubbio lay at the feet of the humble Francis. The solution was bread and meat. All the townspeople had to do was to give the wolf shelter, food, water, and companionship.

Dogs today behave like the wolf of Gubbio. The way we treat them is the way they learn to behave. If we play tug-of-war with them, they learn that we want them to use their teeth when interacting with us. But if your dog is a service dog or a therapy dog, you would refrain from that behavior. The behavior you encourage would be for the dog to lie down by a person and appreciate a soft touch. Another behavior to encourage would be for the dog to fetch his or her own leash or a medical bag. When Rin Tin Tin, the famous German shepherd, was trained, the most important exercise was to retrieve tennis balls in the snow.

One of the finest service dogs that Bolt and I learned from taught us a "down, stay," with a treat on top of each paw (hold) until you say "Free" and your dog eats the treats. This way, the dog learns not to roughhouse with humans or other dogs. In addition, Bolt was never kept in a cage. Trainers do differ on this topic. The main point of most great dog professionals is to choose your methods, ignore other people's opinions of your dog, and never let anyone touch or influence your dog. Like Francis of Assisi's "Wolf of Gubbio," only you and your dog know the truth between you. What he weighs, who he is, how calm he is. How your dog sees the world and how he sees you are all part of the construct that forms as soon as your relationship begins.

Francis of Assisi, born into a noble house, learned to read, write, play the mandolin, and sing and fraternize with other nobles in his town. He served in the military, in the war with Perugia, and was held prisoner and released at the end of the conflict. The young man Francis also exhibited proficiency in horsemanship.

The harshness of the divisions in society during this era in the Middle Ages called for many changes before a rebirth of ideas in science, math, the arts, and sociology, called the Renaissance, could begin (Shaw, *Introduction*). The day in his life when Francis of Assisi listened to his heart and followed his faith and devoted his life to God's call, the change in him towards the remainder of his life began. Francis of Assisi left his rich life as Giovanni de Pietro do Bernardone, took up the name Francis, and challenged the higher class, raising the poor in theory to equal status (Vickrey, Lecture, 2015). The Sermon on the Mount became a literal guide, as did every word Jesus of Nazareth had shared. Francis gave up worldly goods, founded an order based on humility, chastity, and poverty, and offered many writings and traditions that people of all classes could understand, including Christmas carols, mangers, and poems. Francis himself walked to the Holy Land to negotiate and bring an end to the Fifth Crusade. To this day Franciscans care for the holy places there, as appointed by the leader with whom Francis met.

One poem Francis wrote that rings praise in many cultures is titled "The Canticle of Brother Sun and Sister Moon," written in 1224 (Uglito 33–56). The piece speaks of seeing beyond our own pain, challenges our inner self: the sun's warmth on our face and the moon's gentle light at night. Francis told of how we can be so concerned and consumed with our own scars that we cannot see or feel God's great gifts to us, the simple beauty around us. Francis points out that if we can just step out of ourselves and let happiness and peace enter our hearts through experiencing the wonders of nature, we can begin to let go of our inner pain. Again, this is a reflection of the Beatitudes, also known as the "Sermon on the Mount."

Cumulatively, Francis of Assisi's effect on the human experience and the development of civilization resulted from a combination of his education, providing creative and intellectual development during his upbringing, and his clear, unswerving faith in the path. His God provided for him. Francis followed the words in the Bible literally, and started a movement that raised the serfs, or poorest of the population, to the status of deserving equal status in the eyes of God and man—when the poor began to be seen as they are defined in the Beatitudes. For centuries, scholars have painted to these facts as part of the catalysts that spurred society into the Renaissance. Therein lies the heart of hermeneutics and poetics in the works and life of Francis of Assisi. They exist in his simplified interpretation of following the way of peace illuminated in Christ's life.

The minstrel, the poet, the man of peace who ended a crusade without violence, the holy man Francis of Assisi, who tamed the wolf of Gubbio and showed us a diplomatic path to a better life, is still relevant today. Franciscan-centered meditation heals pain and effectively helps anxiety. Further research will show many benefits. And if we listen closely, I am sure somewhere there is always a carol or two on the wind, celebrating in the manner of the minstrel man from Assisi (Walsh).

Works Cited

Brunforte, Ugolito, and Raphael Brown. *The Little Flowers of Saint Francis.* Image Books, 1958.

Shaw, George Bernard. *Saint Joan.* Penguin Classics, New York, 2001.

Vickrey, John F. Lecture Spring, 2015, "Saint Joan: A Play." George Bernard Shaw.

Walsh, P. Jacques. *Maritain Center: Greatest of Centuries, XVI,* "Francis the Saint, The Father of the Renaissance." Maritain.nd.edu/jmc/etext/walsh-p.htm. Accessed 9 Aug. 2019.

Chapter 11

Narrative Hermeneutics

Dr. Maryann P. DiEdwardo

Lehigh University;
University of Maryland Global Campus

Central to the study of hermeneutics is archival study. My research relies on self-examination and self-study, with research practices based on primary sources. My research offers my readers a concentration on curiosity, solitude, and self-development through writing. I am a representation of the themes in my paper: interior self, humility, and complexity. Reading letters and archival evidence advocating human rights is a methodology. The conceptual frameworks of the metaphysics of presence (deconstruction) and metaethics (ethos) seek to resolve questions of human morality by defining concepts such as good and evil, virtue and vice, and justice and crime by evaluating settings or localities in literature. For example, ethical placelessness put upon refugees violates human rights.

Action-based events such as citizen-generated participatory events, in the space of an area near the Lehigh River overlooking South Mountain, provide places for reflection and for nonviolent social interaction to support human rights. I study online with the M. K. Gandhi Institute for Nonviolence in Rochester, New York. The theoretical basis for this chapter and argument center on continued efforts in social pedagogy, to seek peace through defining, researching, and practicing civic values. The research focused on the cultural landscape of specific literary works and associated activities advocate evidence-based change.

Hermeneutics calls for action. As such, service writing and volunteering at local and regional, as well as national community engagement events, inspire diversity, multiculturalism, tolerance, human rights, and civic values. My mission has been service to local soup kitchens and domestic abuse centers, delivery of food for soup kitchens, caring for the sick, and befriending those in need. First, when the author walks in and sees the empty soup kitchen at Trinity Episcopal Church, Bethlehem, PA, she notices a large space with tables and chairs. But when the workers arrive and begin to make the meals, we join together to serve.

Also, thoughts on literacy apply to knowledge of mechanisms that form writing goals. Writing is a human right. Archives are primary sources. Letters, excerpts of evidence, survive to share moments of humanity. Journals share inner life. Art is essential as a space to view human creative instinct, as are short fiction and novels. I use the art gallery teaching collection to teach immigration too. The lower gallery at Lehigh University Art Galleries had a collection of Latin American art. Emphasize intrapersonal and interpersonal study of immigration or resistance to immigration. Visit alternative perspectives on religious beliefs, economic status, and the role of women.

Narrative hermeneutics is my approach to researching the social critic and supporter of human rights, Thomas Merton, an important writer of the American literary tradition. Exegesis, though, often used in conjunction with the textual analysis of Scripture, refers to the interpretation and analysis of any text. Upon the death of Thomas Merton on December 10, 1968, at a monastic meeting on interreligious monastic life in Bangkok, the exegesis of his works have become a global phenomenon. His funeral was held in the Abbey of Gethsemani near Bardstown, Kentucky, on December 17, 1968. By seeking to find connections in the works of Merton, I eventually return to my own journaling and my prayer journaling as well, to reconstruct my own writing as a peaceful endeavor.

The action research case study, *The Significance of the Writing of Thomas Merton,* gathers qualitative research. The purpose of the project centers on my own desire to share a lifetime of wonder and motivation from reading works by Thomas Merton. As a child, I was introduced to Merton's autobiography, a capstone literary piece paramount to my study. When reading his works, I made annotations which are interwoven in my prayer journals. During the period of the case study, I recorded dates and specific readings from the works of Thomas Merton. Upon key passages, I reflected with prose, sketches, original poetry, and contemplative practices. The schedule for the case study often began at 5:00 AM. I not only remained consistent with my routines at home, but also served in a volunteer capacity in area communities to study civics and social and community workshops on practical applications, to apply my knowledge from contemplative study and to cultivate peace. Yet, moving forward with contemplative prayer as a daily devotion, twice a day or more, changed me. The case study results contain both a miraculous healing of my lumbar spine and growth in contemplative prayer to cultivate peace.

My case study may be helpful for creating new perspectives into opportunities for actions concerning faith, service, or a contemplative life.

My hermeneutic arc includes Finding Your Voice, Analytical, Descriptive; Developing Your Research Policy Argument; 3000 or more words. MLA Style and Advocacy. Narrative hermeneutics will use metacognitive practices to use in traditional, hybrid, and distance classrooms. Develop student-directed pedagogical strategies and 21st-century pop culture themes to ignite a learning community for reflection, discovery, and self-efficacy to motivate writers. Focus on Multiple Intelligence Theory, Life Story Writing, Studying Oral Histories, Writing Process Theory, Learning Paradigm, and Learning Communities. Gain knowledge of applications of the aspects of models, paradigms, and frameworks that apply metacognitive pedagogy to create best practices.

Applications of models, paradigms, and frameworks with metacognitive pedagogy create best practices. In 2003, my original case study research connected music and linguistic intelligences to suggest that modern music lyrics as a catalyst improve self-efficacy and thesis design. My original metacognitive framework employs creative processes to offer transformation. Stories that students create in the new literature of the social network become the new voices for a global cultural literature revolution. Mirror the classroom by following activities that students can perform before they enter the classroom. The takeaway is a designed curriculum integrating research findings with participants' views and knowledge.

Chapter 12

The Poetic Vision of Emily Dickinson:
A Case Study

Dr. Maryann P. DiEdwardo

Lehigh University;
University of Maryland Global Campus

Introduction and background

Can one heal from grief by reading the poetry of Emily Dickinson? From the perspective of hermeneutic interpretation, consider the impact of writing journal entries of short reflections and poetry as a methodology to create personal and poetic embodied space, the location where human experience and consciousness takes on material and spatial form. Apply a hermeneutic approach to interpret poetry by writing original poetry. The actions of essential criterion of hermeneutic study use text, respect for history by the author of the text, and consider the significance of the text. To prepare for this book and to engage in primary source research for a qualitative research study, this researcher performed a case study research project. The importance, therefore, in experiencing the aesthetic of the writing of poetry is one of literary hermeneutics. The case study allows the researcher to investigate a single participant in far more detail. Data is gathered by using the nomothetic approach. Researchers classify people into groups, establish principles, and establish dimensions. This approach uses observations over a period of time to obtain quantitative data. Create predictions about people in general. Limitations may not apply to all individuals. The poems that she read during the twenty-nine days: "Exaltation Is the Going"; "I Never Hear the Word Escape"; "Success Is Counted Sweetest"; "Some Things That Fly There Be"; "To Fight Aloud Is Very Brave"; "An Altered Look About the Hills"; "I Taste a Liquor Never Brewed"; "Safe in the Alabaster Chambers"; "Hope Is the Thing with Feathers"; "I Like a Look of Agony"; "I'm Nobody! Who are You?";" I Felt a Funeral in My Brain"; "There's a Certain Slant of Light"; "The Soul Selects Her Own Society"; "Some Keep the Sabbath Going to Church"; "I'll Tell You How the Sun Rose"; "What Soft Cherubic Creatures"; "I Heard a Fly Buzz When I Died"; "A Bird Came Down the Walk"; "I Died for Beauty, But Was Scarce"; "The Heart Asks Pleasure First"; "It Was Not Death, for I Stood Up"; "If You Were Coming in the Fall"; "I Like to See It Lap the Miles"; "It Makes No Difference Abroad"; "The Brain Is Wider Than the Sky"; "I've Seen a Dying Eye"; "I Ask No Other Thing"; "Because I Could Not Stop for Death"; (Dickinson, Emily 14–47).

Excerpts of seven reflections and seven poems by the single subject, myself, are presented with the date, the reflection, and the poem.

Entry 1. February 24, 2019. The single subject read "Exaltation Is the Going" by Emily Dickinson. Reflection: Going to the next life in the Lord takes me to where I dream. I have always been loving. I learned love. As a child, I loved to be around images of Jesus and church. So I naturally tend to ponder grace and peace.

Poem 1

On Mom's anniversary of death,
I mourn and feel the same sadness,
shadows and cold.

Entry 2. February 25, 2019. The single subject read "I Never Hear the Word Escape" by Emily Dickinson. Reflection: My soul is free. But when I read poetry, my spirit and soul rejoice in the life that I have now. I wonder if escaping to death will be any different? Who will I meet? Will my dearest loving family greet me when I pass away?

Poem 2

The time I go away will be alone
Go, go away death
Come, come life
Forever will I love this place
My earthly home afar
Yet close is my joyous presence.

Entry 3. February 26, 2019. The single subject read "Success Is Counted Sweetness" by Emily Dickinson. Reflection: My father was a prisoner of war who makes me wonder about the nearness of success as a reaching, wanting sacrifice. The poem by Dickinson scatters thoughts away from the material world and goes right to the metaphysical. A wanting for the dream is sweet. The dream is painful, in death. But the wanting may be better when we look back. We see death as a new awakening of the energy of the light of the longing. The longing for the desire may be the understanding. He walked the Black March in World War II and starved unless he could sneak tree roots for survival.

Poem 3

Go to the march, the Black March of death.
Eat the tree roots, but walk the path.
No, war is away from home and peace;
the tree roots had been the food beneath.

Entry 4. February 27, 2019. The single subject read "Some Things that Fly There Be" by Emily Dickinson. Reflection: I wish for the glorious third verse every day and miss my loved ones, but cherish the strife in this poem. It makes me quiet and soulful, but happy with the love we can feel in the fullness of afterlife, a gracious and kind vision.

Poem 4

A riddle about flying creatures,
a second about staying in grief, holds truth.
Grief never fades, but the risen souls are analogous to the skies.

Entry 5. February 28, 2019. The single subject read "To Fight Aloud Is Very Brave" by Emily Dickinson. Reflection: The snow imagery is stunning.

Poem 5

Fight. Never in snow.
For snow is silvery and pure.
The fight ends with the melting snow.

Entry 6. March 1, 2019. The single subject read "An Altered Look about the Hills" by Emily Dickinson. Reflection: The poem is unexpected. The poet is on a poetic journey.

Poem 6

The soft light of snow
upon the tree, is calming,
encourages me.

Entry 7. March 2, 2019. The single subject read "I Taste a Liquor Never Brewed" by Emily Dickinson. Reflection: The poem is playful.

Poem 7

Nor do I drink … I am contemplative.

Analysis, evaluation, and recommendations

The criterion for the analysis will be based on the hermeneutic arc of poetic and aesthetic praxis that the author has developed during this study. The poetic and aesthetic knowledge of the author and the poet are the paramount criterion. The ability to reflect and to write original poetry is the other criterion. The actions of essential criterion of hermeneutic study use text, respect for history by the author of the text, and consider the significance of the text. The results of the study demonstrate that the single subject wrote original poetry and reflections based on reading the poetry of Emily Dickinson. The results of Maryann DiEdwardo's case study may reveal that respect for the history of the poetry is revealed in the reflections. The creative original poetry does not combine inquiry and systematic methods of interpretation as the original goals of the case study. Instead, the poems reveal a practice of writing that shows different styles, such as a blues poem (Poem 3) and a haiku (Poem 6). Methodology in the case study uses the poetry of Dickinson for inquiry and interpretation of the events and conditions of daily life. Observations that the single subject may have healing from grief follow. The subject wrote about the losses in her life. The time period of the case study was the year when her parents had passed away in 2006 and 2008. The poetry uses metaphors and imagery from the single subject's experiences as she relates to her sadness over the deaths of her parents. She recognized her grief. Reading, reflecting, and writing poetry was an approach to engage in interpreting the self. Possibly, hermeneutics and phenomenology join to create aesthetic praxis. The limitations are the shortness of reflections and poems by the single subject. The case study may only observe the single subject. The results of the case study suggest that the researcher reinvents her devotion to the study of poetry.

Works Cited

Dickinson, Emily. *Great American Poets*, Emily Dickinson. Edited by Geoffrey Moore, New York: Potter, 1986.

Chapter 13

New Utterances, the Overmind, and Moments of Being: Three Modernists Reach Beyond Ordinary Consciousness

Jill Kroeger Kinkade

University of Southern Indiana

Modernism, as a movement, brought new forays into art, philosophy, architecture, and literature. Freudian Psychology, in its infancy, was being explored by non-analysts and non-analysands alike—by ordinary laypeople of a certain class and intelligence. People—especially writers in Europe—were reading, thinking, talking and writing about the mind in a critical way. Some of these works have become seminal in Western Thought, some have been forgotten, and some though read infrequently have left a significant contribution to 20th-century letters. Many modernist writers were exploring the unconscious to nurture their creative lives. And sometimes their quests look downright zany, as if closing one eye halfway to see differently. And sometimes, Vision in poets can indeed seem like madness to the rest of the world. Such vision is celebrated in this chapter about three writers who explored consciousness in their fiction and nonfiction works: D. H. Lawrence, Hilda Doolittle (hereafter H.D.), and Virginia Woolf.

In D. H. Lawrence's *Fantasia of the Unconscious* (1922), he strikes at a new aesthetic, in which we should "rip the old veil of a vision across, and find what the heart really believes in, after all: and what the heart really wants, for the next future. And we've got to put it down in terms of belief and of knowledge. And then go forward again, to the fulfillment in life and art" (16). Lawrence calls his vision a pseudo-philosophy and says his critics might call it "Pollyanalytics" (15). He isn't going to try to convince anyone of anything, it goes against his nature. The Forward to *Fantasia* is quite funny. While slightly defensive about what readers will think and feel, write and say, he is going to write his new vision, regardless, "And if I try to do this—well why not? If I try to write down what I see—why not?" (16). Though he claims his readers may see this work as a "revolting mass of wordy nonsense" (11), he asserts it anyway. He writes about a metaphysical vision that unfolds into life and art. And though he is stammering "out the first terms of a forgotten knowledge" he claims that what he can do, rather than revive kings or old science, is to use the memory of these—science and sages—as an impetus to "develop a new living utterance. The spark is from dead wisdom, but the fire is life" (14). A new living utterance.

Lawrence breaks with Freud by saying that though sex is important, it is not everything. Lawrence "… associates sex with creativity of the soul. For him, sex becomes a way of connecting with all life—it can be transcendent" (Sklenicka 164). And he values what he calls "subjective science," something that can be learned through experience and intuition, to which all people have access. Lawrence writes about the world's aboriginal peoples, their symbols and myths, and how deep down they are similar, saying that "the great myths all relate to one another" and have the capacity to hypnotize us once again. Lawrence echoes Jung's "Collective Unconscious" when he writes about "the intense potency of symbols is part at least memory" (*Fantasia of the Unconscious* 155). Lawrence goes on to say that he does "not believe in evolution, but in the strangeness and rainbow-change of ever-renewed creative civilizations" (xii).

Ed Jewinski, in his article, "The Phallus in D. H. Lawrence and Jacques Lacan," looked at Lawrence through a Lacanian lens, noting that Lawrence was the first "English writer to reject the humanist notion of the self and compares this rejection with Lacan's concept of *difference*" (cited in Sklenicka 165). Carol Sklenicka, however, in her book *D. H. Lawrence and the Child* asserts that the two writers have in mind very different things when referring to the phallus— Lacan undermining "humanism by insisting upon the constructed nature of language and the human subject" while Sklenicka sees Lawrence "challeng[ing] humanistic assumptions about the human spirit by insisting upon its (pre-linguistic) basis in the body" (165).

Lawrence's concept of "Blood Consciousness" hearkens back to the "felt science" from experience and intuition, and in it he looks at the solar plexus (heart? gut?) and the lumbar ganglion (groin?) as more foundational areas of the human being which we should follow rather than the mind. Knowing through the blood, for Lawrence, is preferable to Knowing through the intellect. To him, mankind had gotten so far away from its true (animal?) nature, that we need to right the imbalance. His writing, (fiction and nonfiction), further this philosophy: "The final aim is not to *know*, but to *be*," Lawrence asserts (68). In this way, Lawrence's belief system recollects Buddhist and Hindu religions. And he calls for all schools to be closed at once! Education is part of the deadening influence of civilization on man, he says, and has prevented original thoughts, original utterances (69). Lawrence goes on: "Yet we *must* know, if only in order to learn not to know. The supreme lesson of human consciousness is to learn how *not to know*. That is, how not to *interfere*. That is, how to live dynamically, from the great Source, and not statically" (99). He continues, "At last, knowledge must be put into its true place in the living activity of man. And we must know deeply, in order even to do that" (99). In other words, he asserts humans need to get out of our heads more, and into our bodies and souls.

In *D. H. Lawrence and the Body Mystical*, published in 1932, Frederick Carter, a friend of Lawrence's, writes "more than ever now, it is necessary for some strong voice to declare that the mystic seeks, simply, the method of approach in man's intimate relation with the universal" (7). Part of the mysticism of Lawrence, according to Carter, was the "Adam-ness" of man, if you will, "That was Man, the primal, original, self of his self" (14). Going within and down deep, into his soul, involving the ganglia and the groin and the blood and the solar plexus involved a dynamic maleness (my term) that was to feed Lawrence's creativity. Salvation, for Lawrence, was not to be found in another world, but to be found in this life, by a "revivifying descent within one's self. Such a regenerative ceremonial was not otherworldly but was close-knit into this life. It meant more and fuller life here" (Carter 16). Our prisons are old habits (16). Lawrence looked at the occult, at astronomy, at the Vedas, at Buddhism, Christianity, the Kabbalah, the macrocosm of the cosmos, the microcosm of man, and read copiously to formulate his theories. So, while he is minimizing the importance of reason and the intellect, he is using these very well to make his points. We can never move outside of the world of signs and symbols, though we can interrogate them.

As Rachel Blau DuPlessis has written in *H.D.: The Career of That Struggle*:

> "This Otherness can never 'truly' be spoken" (37). Although DuPlessis is writing about H.D. and her exploration of Otherness in a female writing sense, this vision of the poet as Seer is often beyond language and intellect. Further, Lawrence writes, "To be alone with one's own soul. Not to be alone without my own soul, mind you. But to be alone with one's own soul! This, and the joy of it, is the real goal of love. My own soul, and myself. Not my ego, my conceit of myself. But my very soul. To be at one in my own self. Not to be quoting any more. Not to be yearning, seeking, hoping, desiring, aspiring. But to pause, and be alone" (*Fantasia* 197).

Hilda Doolittle (H.D.) explored the occult and moved from her deeply devout Christian Moravian family and identity—outsiders from the beginning—in Bethlehem, Pennsylvania, to Ezra Pound calling her Dryad—a tree nymph. Her vision was a mystical combination of (among other schools) psychoanalysis, feminism, and mythology. Her regeneration occurs through seeing anew and reshaping her world through that new vision. H.D. explores her own aesthetic vision and creative process in *Notes on Thought and Vision*.

Written in 1919, when Bryher (her friend and later life mate) had taken H.D. to the Scilly Islands, off the coast of Cornwall, as Albert Gelpi, in his introduction to the 1982 City Lights Books edition writes, "to rest and rise again from the wreckage of the previous five years H.D. found herself in every respect, *in extremis* on unknown boundaries and strange thresholds" (7). It is here that H.D. formulates a poetic vision of her creative process that at times seems a recording of a psychic break. It is here she had her jellyfish experience. She writes if she could describe the overmind: "in my own case, I should say this: it seems to me that a cap is over my head, a cap of consciousness over my head, my forehead, affecting a little my eyes. Sometimes when I am in that state of consciousness, things about me appear slightly blurred as if seen under water …" (18). H.D. here appreciates that fuzzy vision, out of focus, separate, rarefied. Her overmind is like "a closed sea-plant, jellyfish, or anemone" into which "thoughts pass, and are visible, like fish swimming under clear water" (18–19). She describes the "the swing from normal consciousness to abnormal consciousness" as being "accompanied by grinding discomfort of mental agony" (*Notes on Thought and Vision* 19). This grinding discomfort may be familiar to others engaged in creative process. It is to me.

H.D. goes on to say that there are feelers on this metaphorical jellyfish, long tentacles of feeling, that extend out from the grey matter of the brain (19). Further, she states "The brain and the womb are both centres of consciousness, both equally important" (21). She also states that anyone can reach this state, not just women, and that "every person must work out his own way" (23). H.D. writes that the mind becomes the body, and the overmind becomes the brain when someone is engaged in artistic endeavors or other creative enterprises (like science) for days (18). Here she is trying to lay out how this creative process manifests in her life; to describe the nearly indescribable creative consciousness.

Albert Gelpi states: "She knew all too well the dangers in her psychic vulnerability to periodic breakdowns, but her unusual susceptibility also made possible a breakthrough into heightened consciousness. The importance of 'Notes on Thought and Vision' is that it anticipates a lifetime spent in the divination of such epiphanal 'spots of time'" (9). H.D. had experienced much trauma in the previous five years, including having had a miscarriage, losing a brother in WWI, losing her father, being disheartened by D. H. Lawrence with whom she had a spiritual passion, being married to non-monogamous Richard Aldington, them breaking up, getting pregnant by Cecil Gray, who wanted nothing to do with the child, and the horrible trauma of World War I in Europe.

She was at the breaking point. The doctors thought neither she nor her baby would survive, but both lived, and it was just two months after all this that Bryher, H.D., and the infant Perdita went to the Scilly Islands, off the Cornish Coast in England.

Ezra Pound, who had been a close friend of H.D. in Pennsylvania, had signed her work "H.D., *Imagiste.*" Pound had been an early supporter of her work, and in his own modernist philosophy, asked writers to "Make it New." Rachel Blau DuPlessis, in *H.D.: The Career of That Struggle* asserts that H.D. was pushing against the *Imagiste* title in numerous books, that a feminist vision was becoming clearer and that H.D. was more connected with her own mystic vision than by being named or desired by other male modernists. It is at this time, around 1919, when H.D. is freed from her close attachments to Aldington, Lawrence, and Pound, and I think not coincidentally helps move H.D. into a space where she can feel/think/be/see/write her own poetic consciousness. She is throwing off the shackles of ownership, of being appropriated by men, and coming into her own Vision.

H.D. begins to have a series of mystical visions and intense dreams and her exploration of those and the thoughts that came after, helped fuel her writing for a considerable time. She would be writing through her trauma in works for much of her life, but she would also be looking at the power of naming, of self-agency, and of creative regeneration. Some of this creative regeneration would occur through sex. But while she is looking at the male/female union, the sperm and the egg union, she is also exploring the "Otherness" of being a woman and being a bisexual woman. And in an interesting prequel to *écriture feminine*, she explores what it is to be a woman writer and to have consciousness in her womb. DuPlessis writes, "While on the one hand, *Notes* concerns a conjoined male and female elite, on the other, female ways of knowing through the female body are privileged accessed points for transformative vision. Sexual energy (the love brain) and psychic understanding (the overbrain) are 'capable of' a special form of thought or 'vision'" (DuPlessis 40, *Notes* 22). Much like Lawrence's Blood Consciousness, H.D. sees consciousness throughout the body and sex as sacred expression.

In "Notes on Thought and Vision," H.D. explores the unconscious, the border between the real and the Imaginary; the mystic and the mundane. She terms what she calls "the overmind" of creativity and that safe place from which she creates. She looks at the connections between subjectivity and objectivity and the real. She looks at the unconscious and various states of consciousness. To her, the creation of art becomes mythic as it does to Lawrence. One can see this as she relates to both Helen of Sparta and Sappho of ancient Greece in her poetry. And she mythologizes herself to flower into the artist she believes herself to be. It lends her authenticity, authority, and voice. *Notes on Thought and Vision* becomes a very personal aesthetic argument celebrating consciousness and creativity.

Virginia Woolf, too, like Lawrence and H.D., wrote fiction and nonfiction. In her "Sketches of the Past," Woolf looks at, among other things, moments of transcendence—that she calls "Moments of Being" when the individual ego is transcended and "the individual consciousness becomes an undifferentiated part of a greater whole" (Jeanne Schulkind, in her Introduction to *Moments of Being* 18). Like her character Mrs. Dalloway, who has moments when all the finite points of life are dissolved into a great connection with ALL that is, Woolf explores some of these moments in her own life, and their relationship to her creative process.

These "Moments of Being" take us out of our daily lives and into a reverie of altered consciousness, almost like fugue states in which people can connect to something greater than themselves. Although an atheist, these moments were particularly spiritual for Woolf. In "A Sketch of the Past" Woolf writes, "If life has a base that it stands upon, if it is a bowl that fills and fills and fills—then my bowl without a doubt stands upon this memory. It is of lying half asleep, half awake. It is in bed in the nursery at St. Ives …" (65). She describes the waves breaking, the acorn on the pull string of the yellow shade, flowing in the breeze, and her feeling in complete ecstasy. She continues, "… the impression of the waves and the acorn on the blind; the feeling as I describe it sometimes to myself, of lying in a grape and seeing through a film of semi-transparent yell …" (65). Here in this half-asleep, half-awake state, almost meditative, Woolf becomes aware of the world, and her connection to it, even as a child, Woolf describes a perception of bliss through the senses. A sense exploration follows of color, texture, and feeling. For Virginia Woolf, qualia are continuously being explored. Qualia being "the specific nature of our subjective experience of the world" (Lodge 8). Through memory, writing, the senses, and recollection, she not only connects with her past, and the Virginia then, with the Virginia now, but she also goes deeper within and reinforces an identity through her exploration of the unconscious. And she uses these tools to create characters with depth.

For Woolf, unlike Lawrence and H.D., the subconscious is not so much found in her body, at least partially because of repercussions from sexual abuse when she was a child. She writes: "the looking glass shame has lasted all my life" (68). She continues, "Yet this did not prevent me from feeling ecstasies and raptures spontaneously and intensely … so long as they were disconnected from my own body" (68). For Woolf, the rapture of creating is more completely mental and ethereal, not physical.

Woolf writes about most people's average days containing much more nonbeing than being. And she conveys three moments of being at St. Ives when she was young. In one she was fighting with her brother Thoby, and she was about to hit him with her fist, as they had been, and she thought, "Why should I hit this person?" and then put down her arm and let him hit her. Another was when her parents were talking about a friend who had killed himself, and how in a walk later, an apple tree was connected somehow with that suicide. In these instances, she felt hopeless and depressed. In another case, when she looked intently at a flower, in full consciousness, she said, "That is the whole," she felt a deep sense of satisfaction. "I was conscious … that I would in time explain it" (72). "And so I go on to suppose that the shock receiving capacity is what makes me a writer. I hazard the explanation that a shock is at once in my case followed by a desire to explain it" (72). She describes these shocks or blows coming at her from behind the cotton wool of life, (which is like the daily nonbeing or non-seeing), but not without meaning or from an enemy, but "a token of some real thing behind appearances; and I make it real by putting it into words" (72). Here Woolf explains her use of memory and consciousness to illustrate part of her philosophy of writing. Using writing as a means to put things together, to make sense of them, to create, is both a healing tool and a deep connector to all things: "behind the cotton wool is hidden a pattern; I mean that we—all human beings—are connected with this; that the whole world is a work of art; that we are parts of the work of art … we are the words; we are the music; we are the thing itself" (72).

Susan Stanford Friedman, in her excellent *Psyche Reborn: The Emergence of H.D.*, asserts "Woolf believed that the reality of experience was indeed ephemeral, momentary, and ultimately subjective. To capture the essence of human experience, the novelist must not limit himself or herself to rendering human behavior from the outside" (68). To be able to create such strikingly real characters, Woolf knew she had to go within, to go within and experience her own dread, her ambivalence about her father, her idealization of her mother, her own bouts of mania and depression, to see the total picture. After some of these mystical visions, she felt like all was connected.

Friedman goes on to say, "As in H.D.'s poetry, Woolf's theoretic and actual focus was on perception, not action; on the subjective, not the objective. For Woolf, this preference for perception over action was linked to her feminism" (68). In her stream of consciousness writing, she closed in on the process of consciousness in her characters through perception. This going within and seeing connections without, and Deeply Seeing through her own lenses, helped her compassion deepen, and her feminist creative vision sparkle.

Lawrence, H.D., and Woolf looked at history, perception, and memory, in their work to create enduring literary and nonfiction works that ask their readers to look at their own psychology, consciousness, subconscious, and to create anew. Readers for generations have been uplifted and enlightened. Virginia Woolf,

H.D., and Lawrence all used explorations of the mind to excavate their past to be in the present moment, to record their lives and philosophy, to overcome physical and emotional hardships, and to create visions and manifestos of creative process.

Works Cited

Carter, Frederick. *D. H. Lawrence and the Body Mystical.* Folcroft Library Editions, 1981.

DuPlessis, Rachel Blau. *H.D.: The Career of That Struggle.* Indiana U.P., 1986.

Friedman, Susan Stanford. *Psyche Reborn: The Emergence of H.D.* Indiana U.P., 1981.

Gelpi, Albert. "The Thistle and the Serpent." Introduction to *Notes on Thought and Vision.* City Lights Books, 1982.

H.D. *Notes on Thought and Vision.* City Lights Books, 1982.

Jewinski, Ed. "The Phallus in D. H. Lawrence and Jacques Lacan." *D. H. Lawrence Review* 21.1 (1989): pp. 7–24.

Lawrence, D. H. *Fantasia of the Unconscious.* Thomas Selzer, Inc., 1922. Project Gutenberg. (n.d.). Retrieved 22 July 2019, from www.gutenberg.org.

Lodge, David. *Consciousness and the Novel: Connected Essays.* Harvard UP, 2002.

Sklenicka, Carol. *D. H. Lawrence and the Child.* University of Missouri Press, 1991.

Woolf, Virginia. *Moments of Being. 2nd Ed.* Preface by Jeanne Shulkind, Harcourt Brace Jovanovich, 1985.

Chapter 14

Conclusion

Dr. Maryann P. DiEdwardo

Lehigh University;
University of Maryland Global Campus

Memorial to Toni Morrison

Figure 4. Permission for photo of Toni Morrison, American Nobel Prize-winner, credit: Jeremy Sutton-Hibbert-Alamy Stock Photo

To illustrate social justice pedagogy and stylistic writing, teach cultural landscape, place, that mirrors the functionality of the language of metaphor of imaginary places. Writers write about their own cultural experiences in places as a preliminary space practice. Further, writers approach the study of literary works through the language of place or setting. Morrison offers us a vision of a narrative space and the trauma of interior personal space to share the pain of the ghost of a baby in *Beloved*. The text reveals the literary imagination through the context of the speeches by the dead baby; we envision a narrative space. Death becomes the condition or quality that is transferred with aesthetic action and nature. The works of Toni Morrison, with her important scholarship and her commitment to writing, are an important cultural change.

Contributors

Maryann P. DiEdwardo

Maryann Pasda DiEdwardo, B.A., summa cum laude, The Pennsylvania State University; M.A. English, Lehigh University; Doctor of Education, Phi Beta Kappa, Sigma Tau Delta, Mortar Board, Phi Kappa Phi, Kappa Delta Phi, Academy of American Poets is the recipient of Northampton Community College Project Aware Outstanding Service Award. DiEdwardo is a speaker, poet, educator, published author, Adjunct Professor, and recipient of the 2017 University of Maryland University College (now UMGC Global Campus) Stanley J. Drazek Teaching Excellence Award and two Professional Achievement Awards. She was awarded by College English Association with a Professional Achievement Award. CEA awarded DiEdwardo with the Karen Lentz Award for Scholarship at the 2016 College English Association Conference, Denver, Colorado. She teaches English composition and literature for UMGC and acts as a writing coach in Research Methods for Lehigh University Graduate School of Computer Science and Engineering. Research interests include hermeneutics, literacy, metacognition, pedagogy, social justice, student-directed learning, stage history, and writing as therapy. Published works include "Pairing Music and Linguistic Intelligences." Record, vol. 41, no. 3, Spring 2005. Author of memoir *The Legacy of Katharine Hepburn*, DiEdwardo was interviewed by Bertrand Tessier for the documentary *Les Couples Mythiques du Cinema, Katharine Hepburn and Spencer Tracy* (2017).

Juliet Emanuel

Juliet Emanuel is Professor at BMCC/CUNY in the Department of Academic Literacy and Linguistics. She has held positions in the leadership of the Department and continues to do so. With interests focused on language acquisition, pedagogy and studies in post-colonialism, multiculturalism and the diaspora, she contributes to works in the field. She examines these areas through her work in organizations in urban communities. She has just rotated off from the position of Executive Director of the College English Association, a national academic organization after six years of service for which she received the organization's highest award. She is a member of several organizations, serving on their boards or on significant committees.

Jill Kroeger Kinkade

Jill Kroeger Kinkade, M.A., English, University of Louisville, 1997, B.A., Hunter College, summa cum laude, Phi Beta Kappa, New York City, 1995, is a former

Trustee for the College English Association. Major scholarly emphases include Modern British and American Literature, Native American Literature, memory, cognition, consciousness and creativity; minor emphases include African American and Asian American Literature, Philosophy, trauma, healing, Women's Studies and Film. She also writes fiction, creative nonfiction, criticism, poetry, plays and screenplays. She teaches English for the University of Southern Indiana. Recent publications include, "Hilda Doolittle (H.D.) Writing to Create the Self" in *American Women Writers, Poetics, and the Nature of Gender Study*, published by Cambridge Scholars Publishing, UK, 2016. Recent presentations include the following creative nonfiction works at the College English Association Conference: March 2016: Denver, Colorado, "Is-ness is My Business: Or the Time I had a Guest Lecturer in my Capstone Class"; March 2017: Hilton Head Island, South Carolina, "The Kitchen: Vignettes from the Hearth"; April 2018: St. Petersburg, Florida, "Ladybug, Ladybug: Community as Bridge"; March 2019: New Orleans, Louisiana, "Liana of the Mind: Moving from Earth to Sky." Kinkade is deeply connected to her community in Evansville, Indiana, and her family (birth and chosen) around the world.

Dr. T. Madison Peschock

Dr. T. Madison Peschock holds her Ph.D. from Indiana University of Pennsylvania. She has over seventeen years of experience teaching in higher education and has taught at California University of Pennsylvania, Indiana University of Pennsylvania, and other Universities. She currently teaches full-time Ocean County College in Toms River, New Jersey, including the class Introduction to Drama, Literature, and Research Writing. Dr. Peschock's area of expertise is American Literature from 1865–1965 with an emphasis on Southern Literature & Crime Literature. She also specialized in archival research and has used the archives at both The New York Public Library and The Library of Congress to write her dissertation, *A Well-Hidden Secret: Harper Lee's Contributions to Truman Capote's In Cold Blood*, which revealed all of Harper Lee's contributions towards Capote's nonfiction novel. Currently, she is working on an essay about southern literature and Thomas Harris's *Red Dragon*. She has given over a dozen papers at both regional and national conferences and has three publications: "What was Harper Lee's role in writing `In Cold Blood?' Alabama: AL.com. 8 Mar. 2016. Web. 2 June 2016; "Ayad Akhtar's *Disgraced* Proves Worthy of The Pulitzer Prize." *Philological Review* 39.2 2014; "Sister Aloysius' Hypocrisy and Lack of Charity in John Patrick Shanley's *Doubt*." *Pennsylvania English* 35 2014.

Patricia J. Pasda, B.F.A., M.F.A.

Patricia J. Pasda, B.F.A., M.F.A., a presenter for NeMLA 2016 and 2018, is an independent scholar, Lucas film and Disney artist, published author, and an apprentice with Professor John F. Vickrey Professor Emeritus Lehigh University. Her affiliations are The Appaloosa Horse Club, The American Watercolor Water Society, Associate Member, Star Trek Welcommittee, Certificates in Dog Training and Horse Training. Publications include her book on horse training *My Appaloosa: a Journal for Anyone Interested in Understanding Horses, with Bonus Insert on Painting and Drawing Horses*, published by Author House and two chapters "Dian Fossey: Idealist to Realist, Kentucky to Africa" and "Clara Barton That Led Me" in the book *American Women Writers, Poetics, and The Nature of Gender Study* published by Cambridge Scholars Publishing 2016. She has also co-authored the following books with Maryann P. DiEdwardo: *The Horse Keeper: The Healing Gifts of Painting and Writing about Horses*. Infinity Publishing; *The Art of Trees*; *Pennsylvania Voices Book I The Horse Prophet*; *Pennsylvania Voices Book II Appaloosa Visions*; *Pennsylvania Voices Book III Appaloosa Dreams*; *Pennsylvania Voices Book IV The River Keeper*; *Pennsylvania Voices Book V The Legacy of Allison*; *Pennsylvania Voices Book VI Collection of Fiction and Nonfiction*; *Pennsylvania Voices Book VIII The Artist's Sketch Book*; *The Marvelous Nature Alphabet Book*; *Horses about Hope*; *The Passing Light*. Kindle. E-book. 2010; *The Mythic Appaloosa*. Xlibris: Bloomington, 2011. *Short Stories. Sequel to The Passing Light; Nature Journaling for a Peaceful Spirit*. Xlibris: Bloomington, 2011.

Susan Stangeland

Susan Stangeland has a Bachelor's Degree in Equestrian Education from Salem College in West Virginia. She is the business owner of Windy Knoll Farm, a horse boarding facility in Bangor, Pennsylvania. Susan graduated from One Spirit Learning Alliance in June of 2018 and is an interfaith minister. Susan is also a Reiki Master and works out of her home in Bangor, Pennsylvania. Susan is working towards her certification to become an astrologist. She is attending One Spirit Learning Alliance Spiritual Counseling Course and will be graduating as a Spiritual Counselor in 2020.

Bibliography of Works by Dr. Maryann P. DiEdwardo

"Pairing Music and Linguistic Intelligences." *Record*, vol. 41, no. 3, Spring 2005. Kappa Delta Pi, International Education Honors Society.

Spatializing Social Justice: Literary Critiques Maryland: Hamilton Publishing, 2019. *The Significance of the Writing of Thomas Merton, Cultivating Peace.* Philadelphia: FastPencil, 2018. *Transcending Domestic Abuse through the Study and Practice of Writing.* Germany: Lambert Academic Publishing, 2017.

Editor and Contributor. *American Women Writers, Poetics and the Nature of Gender Study.* England: Cambridge Scholars Press, 2016.

Forgotten. Amazon Kindle. E-book, 2016; *Teaching Writing Based on Journaling Concepts of Thoreau.* Amazon. Kindle. E-book, 2015; *Rhetorical Analysis and Metacognitive Pedagogy.* Amazon. Kindle. E-book. 2014; *The White Curtain.* Amazon. Kindle. E-book. 2014; *Adjunct Life.* Amazon. Kindle E-book. 2014; *The Poetry of Landscape after War and Death.* Amazon. E-book. Kindle. 2013; *Restorative Yoga, QiGong, and Tai Chi.* Amazon. E-book. Kindle. 2013; *The Fourth "R": A Book to Promote the Journey through Hispanic American Literary History to Develop Language Skills.* Bloomington, Indiana: AuthorHouse, 2008. Hard copy and e-book; *Music Transforms the College English Classroom.* Hard copy and e-book; *The Legacy of Katharine Hepburn, Fine Art As A Way of Life.* Hard copy and e-book; *Pennsylvania Voices Book IX journaling, blog, wiki, tools for writers; Pennsylvania Voices Book X Writing Based on History: Techniques to Teach Writing through History.*

With Patricia Pasda, co-author: *The Horse Keeper: The Healing Gifts of Painting and Writing about Horses.* Infinity Publishing; *The Art of Trees; Pennsylvania Voices Book I The Horse Prophet; Pennsylvania Voices Book II Appaloosa Visions; Pennsylvania Voices Book III Appaloosa Dreams; Pennsylvania Voices Book IV The River Keeper; Pennsylvania Voices Book V The Legacy of Allison; Pennsylvania Voices Book VI Collection of Fiction and Nonfiction; Pennsylvania Voices Book VIII The Artist's Sketch Book; The Marvelous Nature Alphabet Book; Horses about Hope; The Passing Light.* Kindle. E-book. 2010; *The Mythic Appaloosa.* Xlibris: Bloomington, 2011. *Short Stories. Sequel to The Passing Light; Nature Journaling for a Peaceful Spirit.* Xlibris: Bloomington, 2011.

Honorable Winner. "Hurry." 2015. Allpoetry storywrite.com/contest/2649758-Talk-Geese; Brown Bagazine 4. "Like the Snow." Spring 2008. Tucker, Georgia: *Gypsy Daughter.* Editor, Amy Lynn Hess. www.gypsydaughter.com "Spring

Wind" "Cloud Shadow" "Gentleness" "Friend Frog" "Nutritious Fun" "Anointing" "Daffodil" "Dances" "The Gate" "Soar" were in a book co-authored and illustrated by Maryann Pasda DiEdwardo entitled *Write a Book of Haiku* that was recognized by Dan Poynter and first appeared in 1994. "Joseph" won Honorable Mention, first appeared in *American Poetry Anthology Volume VI*, Number 1, Spring 1986. "Growing Toward Death" semifinalist, first appeared in The International Library of Poetry 2002. "Like the Snow" first appeared in *Pennsylvania Voices Book Three* co-authored and illustrated by Maryann Pasda DiEdwardo 2006. "Rivers" first appeared in Pennsylvania Voices Book Three co-authored and illustrated by Maryann Pasda DiEdwardo 2006. "The Day the Trees Spoke" first appeared in *The Art of Trees* co-authored and illustrated by Maryann Pasda DiEdwardo 2006.

List of Presentations by Dr. Maryann P. DiEdwardo

Center for Teaching and Learning, Lehigh University Symposium. "Hermeneutics, Metacognition and Writing," 2019.

MLA Convention Washington, DC. Chair. "Hermeneutics, Metacognition, and Writing." Presenter of Paper titled "Cultural Landscape in Literature," 2019.

College English Association Conference Presentation "Thomas Merton," 2019.

Southern Atlantic Modern Language Association with College English Association Panel: "Reading to Transgress" Paper Presentation. Birmingham, Alabama. 2018.

College English Association Conference St. Petersburg, FL. "Thomas Merton: Deconstructing Metaphors through the Lens of Derrida in Merton's Elegy about Flannery O'Connor," 2018.

Northeast Modern Language Association. "Examining cultural landscape in literary works presents literary critiques on and reflections of the works of Willa Cather, Ernest Cline, Zora Neale Hurston, Nella Larsen, Flannery O'Connor, Toni Morrison, and Stephanie Powell Watts," 2018.

College English Association Conference. Hilton Head, SC., "Lonely Island of the Self in Feminine Practice in Writing." 2017.

Northeast MLA Baltimore, MD, "Metacognition," 2017.

College English Association Conference, Denver, CO. "Dystopian Architecture in Ready Player One: Semiotic Praxis," 2016.

Northeast Modern Language Association Convention. Hartford, Conn. Chair Women and Gender Studies Panel: presenter of study on the use of place as a sign in "Black Death" by Zora Neale Hurston and "Unassigned Territory" by Stephanie Powell Watts. Also Roundtable speaker for Technology and Innovative Pedagogical Frameworks, 2016.

Northeast Modern Language Association. Selected for Panel Event Leader and Designer. Women and Gender Studies, 2016

NeMLA. Conference. Toronto. "Zombie Archetypes Enliven Creative Nonfiction Writers and Poets." Presenter for Panel as well as presentation entitled "Adjunct Life" for a Roundtable, 2015.

College English Association. Presenter. Moderator. "Poetics, Zora Neale Hurston and Chinua Achebe." Indianapolis, 2015.

"Metacognition, Prezi, Research, and the 21st-Century Scholar." Open Simulator conference.opensimulator.org/2014/program/research-education/ 2014.

Lilly Spring International Conference, Bethesda Maryland. "Metacognition," in June 2014.

College English Association 2014 Baltimore "Metacognitive Pedagogical Models for Literature Study in Higher Education," 2014.

NeMLA NeMLA Convention. 9.23 "The Short Story in the African American Literary Tradition and Authentic Assessment," 2014.

Teleconference Presentations Monthly from July 2012–2013. National QiGong Association Conference. Four Hour Lecture. Philadelphia, PA. "The Efficacy of QiGong," 2013.

Annual Lilly Conference on College and University Teaching – Bethesda, "Writing as a Learning Community to Promote Student Authentic Assessment and Transformation," 2013.

Index

www.ingramcontent.com/pod-product-compliance
Lightning Source LLC
Chambersburg PA
CBHW071136280326
41935CB00010B/1246